NEW WAYS WITH
JELLY ROLLS

NEW WAYS WITH
JELLY ROLLS

12 REVERSIBLE MODERN JELLY ROLL QUILTS

PAM & NICKY LINTOTT

David and Charles

CONTENTS

Introduction

Having written eight best-selling jelly roll quilt books you probably know by now that we love making jelly roll quilts. The basis of all the quilts in our previous books has been that with 'just one jelly roll' you could make any of the quilts. This made things so simple – choose a jelly roll, choose a quilt pattern and away you go! This book, however, is a little bit different.

We love traditional quilts but we also love the look of modern quilts and our latest quilts are certainly being influenced by the modern quilt movement. One of the things we like about contemporary quilts is the negative space for showcasing lots of gorgeous quilting, but we found that when making our quilts we often did not need to use the whole jelly roll. For those who are familiar with our work you know that we don't like to waste fabric, so we have come up

with the perfect solution. For this book we have also pieced our quilt backs and in doing so were able to put any excess jelly roll strips and pieced strip units to very good use. This idea created some stunning quilt backs and we show you how you can do the same. There is a certain freedom when piecing a quilt back – taking this approach allowed us to try something new and be more creative and the end result was that we made a totally reversible jelly roll quilt! We have made our quilt backs approximately 4in larger all round than our quilt tops to allow sufficient fabric if longarm quilting.

We hope you enjoy the quilts in this book, and remember that you can play around with our designs as much as you like. You can look on our patterns as a starting point for creating your own unique designs – there are no boundaries.

Getting Started

What is a Jelly Roll?

A jelly roll is a roll of forty fabrics cut in 2½in wide strips across the width of the fabric. Moda introduced jelly rolls to showcase new fabric ranges. How inspirational to have one 2½in wide strip of each new fabric wrapped up so deliciously! If you want to make any of the jelly roll quilts in this book and don't have a jelly roll to use, then cut a 2½in wide strip from forty fabrics from your stash and you can follow all the instructions in just the same way. Our patterns are based on a jelly roll strip being 42in long.

Imperial or Metric?

Jelly rolls from Moda are cut 2½in wide and at The Quilt Room we have continued to cut our strip bundles 2½in wide. When quilt making, it is impossible to mix metric and imperial measurements. It would be absurd to have a 2½in strip and tell you to cut it 6cm to make a square! It wouldn't be square and nothing would fit. This caused a dilemma when writing instructions for the quilts and a decision had to be made. All our instructions therefore are written in inches. To convert inches to centimetres, multiply the inch measurement by 2.54. For your convenience, any extra fabric you will need, given in the Requirements panel at the start of the quilt instructions, is given in both metric and imperial.

Quilt Sizes

In this book we have shown what can be achieved with just one jelly roll. We have added background fabric and borders but the basis of each quilt is just one jelly roll. The size of our quilts is therefore restricted to this fact but there is nothing to stop you using more fabric and increasing the size of your quilt. The Vital Statistics in each chapter give you all the information you need to enable you to do some simple calculations to make a larger quilt.

Seam Allowance

We cannot stress enough the importance of maintaining an accurate *scant* ¼in seam allowance throughout. Please take the time to check your seam allowance with the seam allowance test at the back of the book.

Tools Used

When cutting half-square triangles from strips, we use the Multi-Size 45/90 from Creative Grids, which has markings that refer to the *finished* size. If you are using a different ruler when cutting half-square triangles, please make sure you are using the correct markings before cutting. For some of the quilts we have also used a large 60-degree triangle ruler that can measure up to 8in triangles.

Diagrams

Diagrams have been provided to help you make the quilts and these are normally beneath or beside the relevant stepped instruction. The direction in which fabric should be pressed is indicated by arrows on the diagrams. The reverse side of the fabric is usually shown in a lighter colour than the right side.

Washing Notes

It is important that pre-cut fabric is *not* washed before use. Save the washing until your quilt is complete and then make use of a colour catcher in the wash, or possibly dry clean.

Before You Start

Before you dive into making a quilt please read all of the instructions fully and don't forget to keep that scant ¼in seam allowance. Most of all – have fun! We designed these quilts to be easy to make and we hope they will be well used and loved. The techniques we use do encourage accuracy but no one is going to be judging you on every last point.

Return to Sender

This striking quilt, with its clean, contemporary layout, is quick and easy to make and uses all but four strips of the jelly roll. We used one of the distinctive ranges designed by V&Co for Moda, which has stunning geometric designs. These fabrics and the geometric layout we used for the quilt creates a very fresh, modern design.

The four spare jelly roll strips were put to good use by making four larger versions of the block and piecing them into the backing fabric to create a totally different, minimalist look on the reverse of the quilt.

Vital Statistics

Quilt size: 52½in x 66in

Block size: 6in x 12in

Number of blocks: 36

Setting: 9 rows of 4 blocks, plus 1½in sashing

Requirements
For quilt top:
- One jelly roll **OR** forty assorted 2½in strips cut across the width of the fabric
- Sashing fabric 1½yd (1.4m)
- Binding fabric ½yd (50cm)

For pieced quilt back:
- Backing fabric 3½yd (3.25m)
- Four spare strips from the jelly roll

Return to Sender Quilt

Preparation

Sorting the jelly roll strips:

- Choose thirty-six jelly roll strips for the blocks and pair up the strips to form eighteen pairs.

- Four jelly roll strips are spare and can be used for the pieced quilt back.

Cutting the jelly roll strips:

- Cut each of the thirty-six jelly roll strips as follows.

  - Two rectangles 2½in x 12½in.
  - Two 2½in squares.
  - One rectangle 2½in x 8½in.

Cutting the sashing fabric:

- Cut twelve 2in strips *lengthways* down the fabric.

- Set eight of these strips aside for the horizontal sashing, which will be trimmed to size later.

- Take the four remaining 2in strips and subcut thirty-one rectangles each 2in x 6½in for the vertical sashing strips.

Cutting the binding fabric:

- Cut six 2½in strips across the width of the fabric.

Making the Quilt

Making the blocks

1 Working with one pair of jelly roll strips at a time, sew the 2½in squares of one fabric to both ends of the 2½in x 8½in rectangle of the other fabric. Press the seams as shown. Sew the 2½in x 12½in rectangles to the top and bottom.

2 Repeat with the remaining fabric to form the second block in the same way.

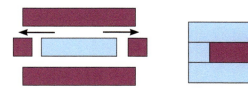

3 Repeat this process with all eighteen pairs of jelly roll strips to create thirty-six blocks.

4 Four blocks need to be cut in half to create half blocks that fit into the ends of rows 2, 4, 6 and 8. After the blocks have been cut in half an extra ½in needs to be trimmed from the top, as shown, to create the right size.

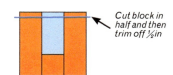

Cut block in half and then trim off ½in

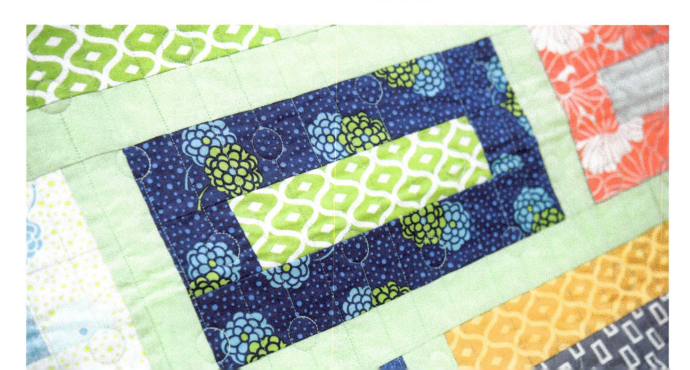

Assembling the quilt

5 Create rows 1, 3, 5, 7 and 9 by sewing four blocks together with three sashing strips in between. Press the seams in the direction shown.

6 Create rows 2, 4, 6 and 8 by sewing three blocks and two half blocks together with four sashing strips in between. Press as shown.

7 Measure the rows and trim the horizontal sashing strips to size. It is important they all measure the same. Sew the rows together with the sashing strips in between. Press the seams.

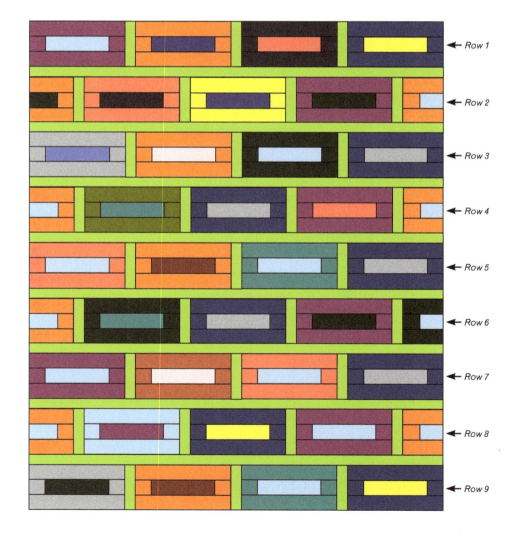

← Row 1
← Row 2
← Row 3
← Row 4
← Row 5
← Row 6
← Row 7
← Row 8
← Row 9

Quilting and finishing

8 Your quilt top is now complete. You can now make a quilt sandwich as normal with your wadding (batting) and backing fabric, ready for quilting. Alternatively, you could piece the back of the quilt as we did by referring to the pieced backing instructions that follow. We made our quilt reversible and incorporated left-over jelly roll strips into our backing.

Tip

You can, of course, use any backing fabric, but remember to make it larger than your quilt front. When longarm quilting we like our backings to be 4in larger on all sides.

9 After quilting, sew the six binding strips into a continuous length and bind the quilt to finish.

We wanted our quilting to reflect the modern nature of our quilt, so we chose a quilting design called Modern Dew Drops by Anita Shackelford, with vertical lines and small circles that continue the geometric theme.

Making a Pieced Quilt Back

Cutting the jelly roll strips

1. Cut each of the four remaining jelly roll strips into the following pieces.
- Two rectangles 2½in x 18½in.
- Two 2½in squares.

Cutting the backing fabric

2. Cut two lengths of fabric each 62in and subcut them as follows for the background.
- Subcut the first length into three rectangles 12½in x 62in *lengthways* down the fabric.
- Subcut the second length into two 7½in x 62in rectangles and four 6½in x 62in rectangles.
- Subcut each of the four 6½in wide strips into one rectangle 6½in x 13in and one rectangle 6½in x 32in.
- From the excess fabric cut four rectangles 2½in x 14½in for the centres of the four blocks.

Assembling the backing

3. Make the blocks in the same way as the blocks for the front of the quilt, using the jelly roll 2½in x 18½in rectangles and 2½in squares and the 2½in x 14½in backing fabric rectangles for the centres of the blocks.

4. Referring to the diagram, sew the backing fabric rectangles together inserting the blocks in the positions shown.

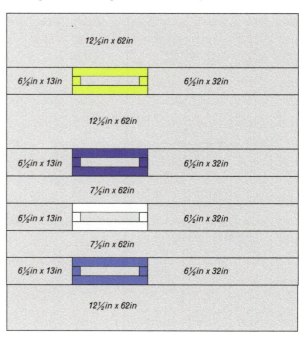

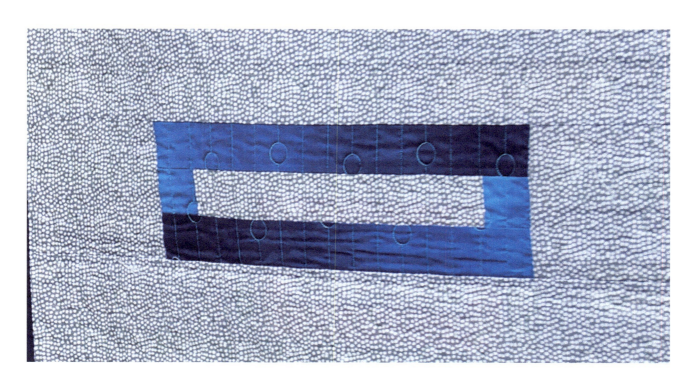

We chose a gorgeous backing fabric in a grey and white pebble design called *Flurry* by Dashwood Studios. We had four jelly roll strips left over from the quilt top and these made up four large blocks using the backing fabric as the centre of the blocks. We liked the fact that the back of our quilt looked sophisticated compared to the fun colours of the quilt top. The quilt front and back were made by the authors and longarm quilted by The Quilt Room.

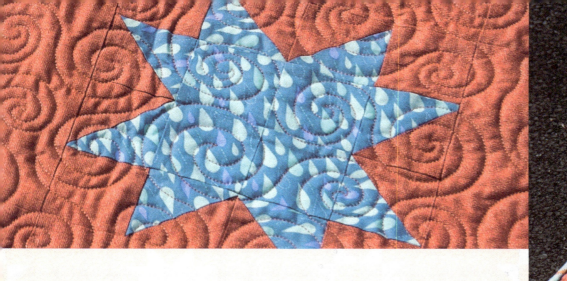

Stars and Stripes

This quilt caused us a dilemma because Nicky preferred the quilt back and would have liked it to be our quilt top. It also used more of the jelly roll strips – twenty-eight strips, whereas our quilt top needed only twelve strips. Our quilt with stars won the day on the basis that it required lengthier instructions – we suppose that's as good a reason as any! It's also a great example of a modern design.

Our quilt back is a brilliant pattern to make and has got to win our prize for the quickest and easiest quilt in the book, yet it still manages to look gorgeous. This is a great example of when you are working with lovely fabrics you can often let them do the work for you! These are called Summertime by Kate Spain for Moda.

Vital Statistics

Quilt size: 56in x 64in

Block size: 8in square

Number of blocks: 28 pieced and 28 solid

Setting: 7 x 8 blocks

Requirements

For quilt top:
- One jelly roll **OR** forty assorted 2½in strips cut across the width of the fabric
- Background fabric 3½yd (3.25m)
- Binding fabric ½yd (50cm)
- Creative Grids Multi-Size 45/90 ruler or other specialist tool for making half-square triangles from strips

For pieced quilt back:
- Backing fabric 2yd (1.75m)
- Twenty-eight spare strips from the jelly roll

Stars and Stripes Quilt

Preparation

Sorting the jelly roll strips:
- Select twelve jelly roll strips and sort them as follows.
- Choose four strips to make twelve 'open' stars (A strips).
- Choose eight strips to make eight 'solid' stars and eight 'open' stars (B strips).
- The remaining strips can be used on the quilt back.

Cutting the background fabric:
- Cut seventeen 2½in wide strips across the width of the fabric.
  - Take five and cut each into sixteen 2½in squares to make eighty. You need 112 in total and the remaining squares will be cut when you are making the half-square triangles from the B jelly roll strips.
  - Leave twelve strips uncut to make the half-square triangles.
- Cut three 4½in wide strips and subcut each strip into eight 4½in squares to make twenty-four. You need twenty 4½in centre background squares, so four are spare. These are the background centres of the 'open' stars.
- Cut seven 8½in wide strips and subcut each strip into four 8½in squares to make twenty-eight in total.

Cutting the binding fabric:
- Cut six 2½in strips across the width of the fabric.

Making the Quilt

Making the open star blocks using A strips

1 Take one jelly roll A strip and a 2½in background strip and press right sides together, ensuring that they are exactly one on top of each other.

2 Lay them out on a cutting mat and position the Multi-Size 45/90 ruler as shown in the diagram, lining up the 2in mark at the bottom edge of the strips. Trim the selvedge and cut the first triangle. You will notice that the cut-out triangle has a flat top. This would just have been a dog ear you needed to cut off, so it's saving you time.

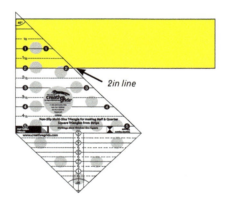

2in line

3 Rotate the ruler 180 degrees as shown and cut the next triangle. Continue along the strip cutting twenty-four triangles in total.

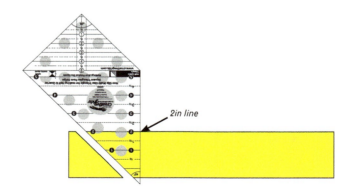

2in line

4 Sew along the diagonal of each pair of triangles. Trim the dog ears. Press twelve of the units towards the jelly roll fabric and twelve towards the background fabric.

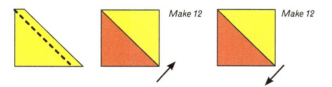

Make 12   *Make 12*

5 Take two half-square triangle units with the seams pressed in opposite directions and, with right sides together, sew together to make a flying geese unit. Pin at the seam intersection to ensure a perfect match. Repeat to make twelve flying geese units in total.

Make 12

6 Sew two 2½in background squares to the ends of a flying geese unit. Press as shown. Repeat to make six.

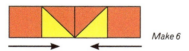

Make 6

7 With the remaining six flying geese units, sew two flying geese units to the sides of a 4½in centre background square. Press as shown. Repeat to make three.

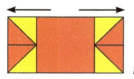

Make 3

8 Sew the rows together as shown to make three open star blocks. Press the seams as shown.

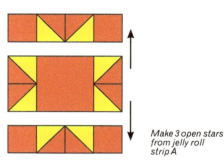

Make 3 open stars from jelly roll strip A

9 Repeat this process with all four A jelly roll strips to make twelve open star blocks. The remaining eight open star blocks will be made from B strips.

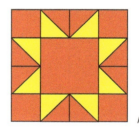

Make 12

Making the closed star blocks using B strips

10 Take one jelly roll B strip and a 2½in background strip and press right sides together ensuring that they are exactly one on top of the other. Cut four 2½in squares from the left-hand side. The four background 2½in squares will be added to the eighty already cut and the four jelly roll squares will make the centres of the closed stars.

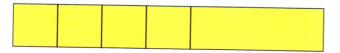

11 Working with the balance of the strips, position the Multi-Size 45/90 as shown in the diagram, lining up the 2in mark at the bottom edge of the strips. Cut the first triangle.

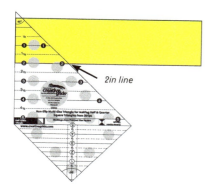

2in line

12 Rotate the ruler 180 degrees and cut the next triangle. Continue along the strip cutting sixteen triangles.

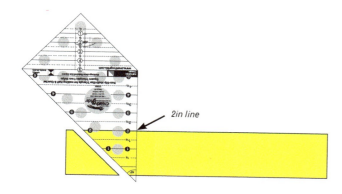

2in line

13 Sew along the diagonal of each pair of triangles. Trim the dog ears. Press eight towards the jelly roll fabric and eight towards the background fabric.

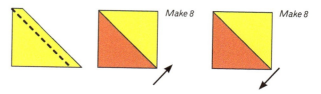

Make 8   Make 8

14 Take two half-square triangle units with the seams pressed in opposite directions and, with right sides together, sew together to make eight flying geese units. Pin at the seam intersection to ensure a perfect match.

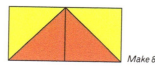

Make 8

15 Sew the four 2½in B jelly roll squares together to make one 4½in centre square.

16 Sew the units and rows together as in steps 6–9 using a 4½in background centre square to make one open star and using the four-patch in the centre to make one closed star.

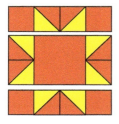 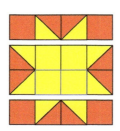

Make 1 open and 1 closed star from each jelly roll strip B

17 Repeat with all eight B jelly roll strips to make eight closed stars and eight open stars. In total you should now have twenty open stars and eight closed stars.

Make 20 in total   *Make 8 in total*

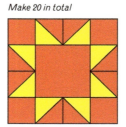 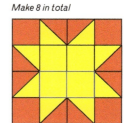

You now have 20 open stars and 8 closed stars

Assembling the quilt

18 Lay out your stars, alternating them with an 8½in background square. When you are happy with the layout, sew the blocks into rows and then sew the rows together.

Quilting and finishing

19 Your quilt top is complete. You can now make a quilt sandwich as normal with your wadding (batting) and backing fabric, ready for quilting. Alternatively, you could piece the back of the quilt as we did by referring to the instructions for a pieced back that follow. You can, of course, use any backing fabric, but remember to make it larger than your quilt. When longarm quilting we like our backings to be 4in larger on all sides.

20 After quilting, sew the six binding strips into a continuous length and bind the quilt to finish.

We chose a quilting design called Deb's Swirls by Deb Geissler, which we quilted densely edge to edge.

Making a Pieced Quilt Back

Cutting the backing fabric

1 Cut three 8½in strips across the width of the fabric for the top and bottom borders.

2 Cut fourteen 2½in strips across the width of the fabric and cut each into two rectangles approximately 2½in x 21in to make twenty-eight in total.

Assembling the backing

3 Take one 2½in x 21in backing rectangle and cut it into two rectangles. These can be random cuts as that is the nature of the design (see diagram). To start off, you could cut it into two equal rectangles 2½in x 10½in.

4 Sew one rectangle to one end of a jelly roll strip and the other rectangle to the other end.

5 Repeat with all twenty-eight 2½in x 21in backing rectangles and the twenty-eight jelly roll strips, varying the sizes of the rectangles you cut, so the piecing has an irregular, stepped look.

6 When you are happy with the arrangement of the rows, sew the rows together.

7 Sew the three 8½in border strips together and then cut in half. Measure from side to side across the centre of the quilt back. Trim the borders to this size and then sew them to the top and bottom of the quilt back to finish.

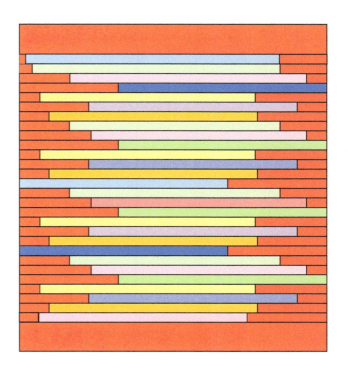

The back of our quilt uses more jelly roll strips than the quilt top, but the instructions are so quick and easy we decided to make it the reverse. If you need a quilt in a hurry then look no further than this pattern. It goes together with ease and with absolutely no wastage. What more could you ask? The quilt front and back were made by the authors and longarm quilted by The Quilt Room.

Cotton Reels

The spools design has always been a firm favourite in patchwork and in this quilt we give it a more modern look, setting the reels within a clean, fresh background. We made three sizes of cotton reels, scattering them across the quilt. Even after allocating eight strips to make a scrappy binding, we had enough strips left over to have fun with the quilt back.

We were lucky enough to have some fat eighths from a lovely range from Tula Pink so decided to create a very modern grandmother's flower garden on the reverse. Our ¾in paper-pieced hexagons are the perfect size to make when working with jelly roll strips and we dotted our flowers randomly around the 'garden paths'. A little hand work is very therapeutic and paper piecing makes a great holiday project.

Vital Statistics

Quilt size: 66in x 78in

Block size: 12in square

Number of blocks: 4 small cotton reel blocks, 2 medium and 3 large, with 7 plain blocks

Setting: irregular, plus 3in border

Requirements

For quilt top:
- One jelly roll **OR** forty assorted 2½in strips cut across the width of the fabric
- Background fabric 4yd (3.75m)
- Binding made from jelly roll strips

For pieced quilt back:
- Backing fabric 4¼yd (4m) in total, although this can be made up of pieces of different fabrics
- Spare jelly roll strips used for making hexagon 'flowers'
- Excess strip units used for making 'garden paths'

Cotton Reels Quilt

Preparation

Sorting the jelly roll strips:
- Choose five navy or dark-coloured jelly roll strips for the cotton reel tops.
- Choose twenty assorted jelly roll strips for the cotton reels.
- Choose eight assorted jelly roll strips for the binding.

Cutting the navy/dark strips for cotton reel tops:
- Cut each of the five 2½in navy/dark strips into four rectangles 2½in x 8½in to make a total of twenty rectangles. You need eighteen, so two are spare.

Cutting the background fabric:
- Cut five 2½in strips across the width of the fabric and then subcut each strip into sixteen 2½in squares to make seventy-two in total.
- Cut seven 3½in strips across the width of the fabric and set aside for the outer border.
- Cut nine 4½in strips across the width of the fabric. Subcut these strips into the following rectangles, cutting the longest rectangles first.
    - Six 4½in x 12½in rectangles.
    - Twenty 4½in x 10½in rectangles.
    - Eight 4½in x 8½in rectangles.
- Cut five 12½in strips across the width of the fabric. Subcut these strips into the following, cutting the longest first.
    - Two 12½in x 36½in.
    - One 12½in x 24½in.
    - Five 12½in x 12½in.

Making the Quilt

Making the cotton reel centre units

1 Take four jelly roll strips and sew them together down the long sides to make one strip unit A. Press the strips in one direction as shown.

Strip unit A – make 1

2 Cut strip unit A into four 4½in unit A segments. The rest of the strip unit is spare and could be used to create 'garden paths' for the quilt back.

3 Sew a 4½in x 8½in background rectangle to both sides of each of the four segments as shown to make four unit A. Press the seams outwards.

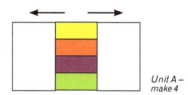

Unit A – make 4

4 Take five jelly roll strips and sew together down the long sides to make one strip unit B. Repeat to make two strip unit B in total. Press the seams in the direction shown.

Strip unit B – make 1

5 Cut each of the strip units into five unit B 4½in segments. You need ten unit B segments in total.

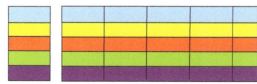

6 Sew a 4½in x 10½in background rectangle to both sides of each of the ten segments, as shown, to make ten unit B. Press the seams outwards.

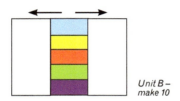

Unit B – make 10

7 Take six jelly roll strips and sew together down the long sides to make one strip unit C. Press the seams as shown.

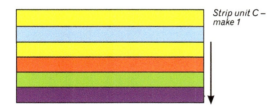

Strip unit C – make 1

8 Cut strip unit C into three unit C 4½in segments.

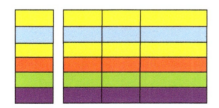

9 Sew a 4½in x 12½in background rectangle to both sides of each of the three segments as shown to make three unit C. Press the seams in the directions shown.

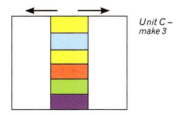

Unit C – make 3

Making the cotton reel top and bottom units

10 Take one 2½in background square and lay it right sides together on a 2½in x 8½in navy rectangle. Sew across the diagonal as shown. If it helps, draw the diagonal line in first or make a fold to mark your stitching line.

11 Flip the square over and press towards the background fabric. Once you have made sure you have sewn the flip-over corner on accurately you can trim the excess background and navy fabric.

Tip

If there is any inaccuracy after you have sewn the flip-over corner it is better not to trim the navy fabric as, although this will create more bulk, it will help to keep your work in shape.

12 Take another 2½in background square and sew it to the other side as shown, pressing and trimming as before. Make eighteen of these units.

13 Sew a 2½in background square to both ends of these eighteen units to complete the cotton reel top.

Make 18

Assembling the cotton reel blocks

14 Sew a cotton reel top to both the top and bottom of a unit A segment, pinning at the seam intersections to ensure a perfect match.

15 Repeat to make four single cotton reels.

Make 4

16 Sew a cotton reel top to one end of a unit B segment, pinning at the seam intersections to ensure a perfect match. Repeat to make ten unit B blocks.

17 Take two unit B blocks and sew together to make a double cotton reel. Repeat to make two double cotton reels in total.

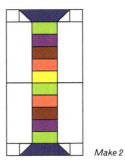

Make 2

18 Take two unit B blocks and sew together with a unit C block in between to make a triple cotton reel. Repeat to make three triple cotton reels in total.

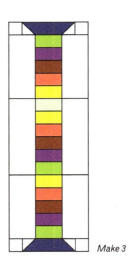

Make 3

Assembling the quilt

19 Referring to the piecing diagram, sew the background squares and rectangles together with the cotton reel blocks as shown.

Adding the border

20 Join the border strips into a continuous length. Determine the vertical measurement from top to bottom through the quilt top centre. Cut two side borders to this measurement. Pin and sew to the quilt. Press seams outwards.

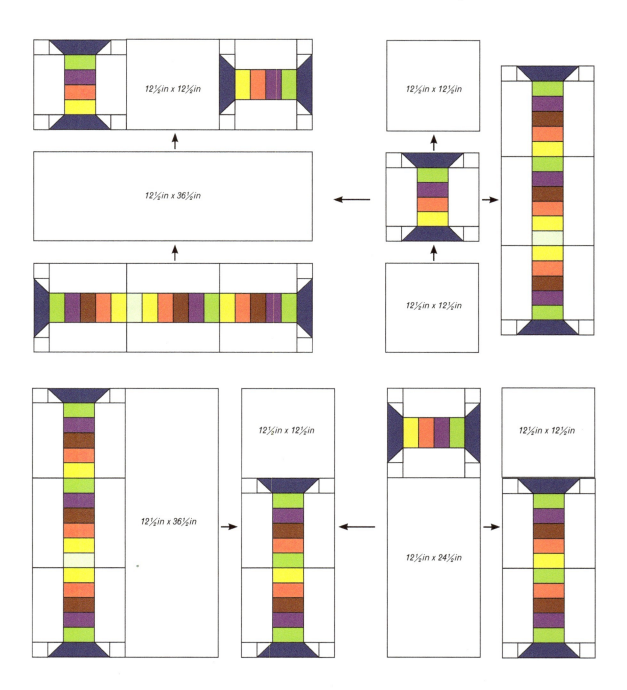

21 Now determine the horizontal measurement from side to side across the centre of the quilt top. Cut two borders to this measurement. Sew to the top and bottom of your quilt and press seams outwards. Your quilt top is now complete and ready for quilting.

Quilting and finishing

22 You can now make a quilt sandwich as normal with your wadding (batting) and backing fabric, ready for quilting. Alternatively, you could piece the back of the quilt as we did by referring to the instructions that follow.

23 After quilting make a scrappy binding by cutting each of the eight binding strips into four rectangles approximately 2½in x 10½in. Sew them into a continuous length, making sure you don't have the same fabrics next to each other.

For the quilting we chose a longarm quilting design with circles running down in vertical rows. The thread used was chosen to blend with the background fabric.

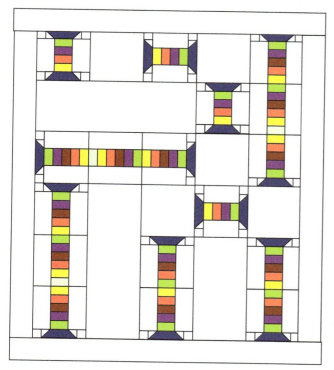

Making a Pieced Quilt Back

Our quilt back is quite random and is meant to resemble a modern grandmother's flower garden quilt. We wanted a little hand work while on holiday and jelly roll strips are perfect when making ¾in hexagons. Jelly roll strips plus some ¾in pre-cut hexagon papers were bundled into our luggage and many a happy evening was spent sewing them together!

When assembling the quilt back, we used some excess pieced strips from the quilt front. These became our 'garden paths' and were inserted into rectangles of backing fabric. We were also lucky enough to have some extra pieces of Tula's fabric, so this was incorporated as well. Six 'flowers' were made in total, each made up of seven hexagons.

It is difficult to give precise instructions for this quilt back as it is meant to be random, so please feel free to do your own thing. We have given instructions for English paper piecing so you can create your own flowers. Our instructions tell you to tack (baste) the hexagons over papers but we speeded things up by using Sew Line Glue, which worked brilliantly. When you come to remove the papers, you can just lift the glued edges and the papers will come out. Choose whichever method suits you.

English paper piecing

1 Make a master template from the full size template given here. It can be traced on to template plastic for a durable master template.

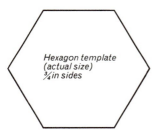

Hexagon template (actual size) ¾in sides

2 One paper template has to be made for every patch. These paper templates must be accurately cut and must be the *exact* size and shape of the finished patch. They can be re-used once the shapes are sewn together and the papers are removed. Copying paper is a good weight. Draw round your master template with a fine marker and cut out accurately along the marked line. Keeping these paper templates accurate is the secret of success. You can of course buy ready-cut paper pieces.

3 Place and pin the paper template to the wrong side of the fabric. Cut the fabric at least ¼in larger all round than the paper piece. This can be judged by eye.

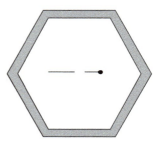

4 Fold the seam allowance over the paper and tack (baste) into position using big stitches, ensuring the corners are carefully folded. Sew right through the fabric and paper with a contrasting thread, so that it can be seen easily for removal later. This is where we used glue instead of tacking thread.

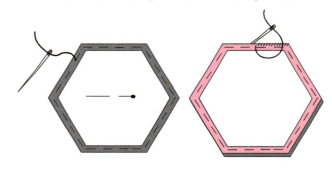

5 To join the patches, place two right sides together and oversew together in a matching thread, catching just the fabric edges. Add the next hexagon in the same way, and so on.

6 When all the pieces are sewn together, press lightly and remove the tacking (basting) thread and papers.

Assembling the backing

7 Assemble all the pieces of your quilt back into a layout that pleases you. Appliqué your flowers into the positions of your choice, using matching thread and tiny slip stitches.

We wanted to have paper-pieced hexagons on our quilt back and we also had some pieced strips left over from the quilt top, which looked like garden paths. The idea of a mixed-up grandmother's flower garden took hold and this is the result. The quilt front and back were made by the authors and longarm quilted by The Quilt Room.

Firecracker

We used a collection of lovely Amish-inspired solids to create this stunning contemporary quilt. The triangle stars create a great sense of rotational movement and the plain colours give the design a modern edge. You do accumulate a number of offcuts when creating the quilt front and we were determined not to waste them, so we used them on the back of the quilt.

Our quilt back is gorgeous and we love it nearly as much as the quilt top. It has a really elegant, modern look, especially with the small, bright triangles against the solid grey background. The design was the perfect solution as no precious fabric was wasted.

Vital Statistics

Quilt size: 43in x 52in

Number of blocks: 35 hexagons

Setting: 10 vertical rows of 7 half-hexagons, plus 6in border

Requirements
For quilt top:
- One jelly roll **OR** forty assorted 2½in strips cut across the width of the fabric
- Border fabric 1yd (1m)
- Binding fabric ½yd (50cm)
- Creative Grids 45/60 ruler or any 60-degree triangle ruler

For pieced quilt back:
- Backing fabric 3yd (2.75m)
- Cut-off triangles from the quilt front

Firecracker Quilt

Preparation

Sorting the jelly roll strips:
- Choose thirty-six jelly roll strips and sort them into eighteen pairs that work well together.

- Four strips are spare.

Cutting the border fabric:
- Cut four strips 6½in wide across the width of the fabric and set aside for the border.

- Cut two 3½in strips across the width of the fabric. Lay the 60-degree triangle ruler on a strip, lining up the 3½in marking along the bottom of the strip and the nubbed-off top of the triangle at the top of the strip. Cut one triangle.

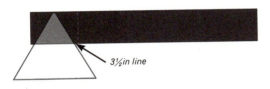

- Rotate the triangle along the strip to cut ten triangles. Repeat with the second strip to make twenty triangles. Set these aside for the top and bottom triangles of each vertical row.

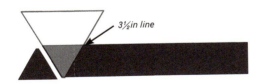

Cutting the binding fabric:
- Cut five strips 2½in wide across the width of the fabric.

Making the Quilt

Making a block

1 Take one pair of jelly roll strips and sew them together to form a strip unit as shown. The top fabric will form the background of the block and the bottom fabric will become the star. Press the seams towards the darker fabric.

2 Cut the strip unit into twelve 3½in segments to make twelve rectangles each 3½in x 4½in.

3 Working with one rectangle at a time, rotate each rectangle 90 degrees to the right so the background fabric is *always on the right*.

4 Place the 60-degree triangle on the rectangle, aligning the 3½in line along the bottom of the rectangle and the nubbed-off top of the triangle with the top of the strip unit. Cut the triangle. Repeat with all twelve rectangles from the strip unit.

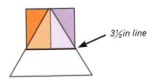

5 The cut off fabric pieces are spare but keep them to one side for your pieced quilt back.

6 Take three triangles and sew them together as shown to make a half-hexagon. Press each unit as shown, before sewing the next unit in place. Repeat with all twelve triangles, to make four half-hexagons. *Do not sew the half-hexagons together to form hexagons at this stage.*

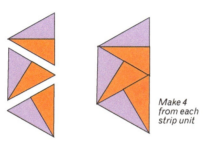

Make 4 from each strip unit

7 Repeat to make four half-hexagons from each of the eighteen strip units to make a total of seventy-two half-hexagons. You need seventy, so two are spare.

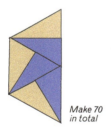

Make 70 in total

Tip

The beauty of this quilt design is that the half-hexagons are sewn together in rows later, avoiding the need for set-in seams.

Assembling the quilt

8 Referring to the quilt diagram, lay out the half-hexagons into vertical rows as shown, making sure you match the half-hexagons carefully so they form full hexagons. Add a background triangle to the top and bottom of each vertical row.

9 When you are sure they are in the right place, sew the half-hexagons into vertical rows. Now sew the vertical rows together, pinning at every seam intersection to ensure a perfect match. Press the seams of alternate rows in opposite directions to help when sewing the seams – there will be occasions when you might have to re-press a seam.

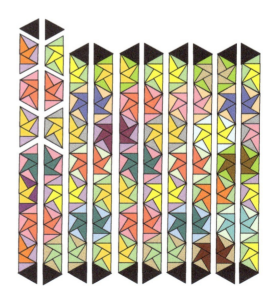

Adding the border

10 Determine the vertical measurement from top to bottom through the centre of your quilt top, measuring from the tip of the hexagon in the top row to the tip of the hexagon in the bottom row. Trim two side borders to this measurement. Pin and sew to the quilt. Press the seams outwards.

11 Determine the horizontal measurement from side to side across the centre of the quilt top. Trim two borders to this measurement. Pin one to the top of the quilt, aligning the sewing line with the top of the hexagons to form a straight edge. Sew and then cut off the excess fabric. Press the seams outwards. Repeat with the border at the bottom of the quilt. Sewing the borders in this order means you do not have any joins in the borders. Your quilt top is now complete and ready for quilting.

We wanted a bold, modern quilting design that would work well on both the front and back of the quilt, so we chose a simple figure-of-eight pattern in a grey thread. The thread really shows in the black borders but does not affect the overall pattern. It also 'melts' into the quilt back and gives our modern quilt a really good texture and depth.

Quilting and finishing

12 You can now make a quilt sandwich as normal with your wadding (batting) and backing fabric, ready for quilting. Alternatively, you could piece the back of the quilt as we did by referring to the instructions that follow.

13 After quilting, sew the six binding strips into a continuous length and bind the quilt to finish.

Making a Pieced Quilt Back

Cutting the backing fabric

1 Cut five 6½in strips and set these aside for the borders of the quilt back.

2 Cut fourteen 4½in wide strips across the width of the fabric and subcut each strip into six rectangles 4½in x 6½in. You need eighty in total, so four will be spare.

Assembling the backing

3 You need to make a template so you can trim the corners of the rectangles to the correct size. To do this, take one of the cut-off triangles and trim ½in from the long side. Discard the ½in strip and the smaller triangle will be your template.

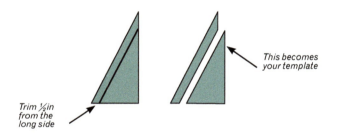

Trim ½in from the long side

This becomes your template

4 Lay the template on one corner of the rectangle and cut away the corner of the rectangle. Repeat on the diagonal corner. We strongly recommend sewing **one** block first, to make sure you are not cutting away too much, because if you cut away too much your cut-off triangles will be too small.

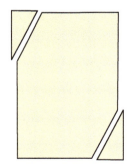

5 Choose a cut-off triangle and with right sides together sew it to the corner as shown. Repeat on the opposite corner and then press. Use a quilting ruler to trim to size. Repeat with all eighty rectangles.

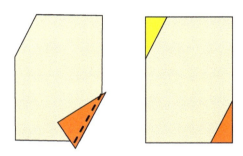

6 Sew eight rectangular units together to form one vertical row. Repeat to make ten vertical rows. Press the seams of alternate rows in opposite directions. Sew the rows together, pinning at every seam intersection to ensure a perfect match.

7 Complete the quilt back by sewing the outer border strips into a continuous length and sewing to the quilt back in the same way as the quilt front (steps 10 and 11).

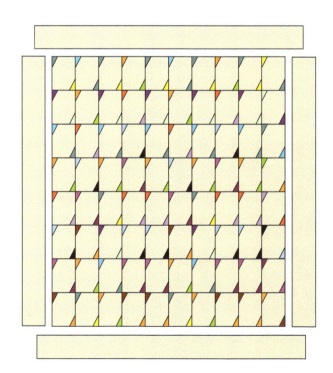

We loved the design of the Firecracker quilt top, however, we did have lots of offcuts from the 60-degree triangles and there was no way we were going to waste them. Our design for the reverse uses them up perfectly and set against a solid pale grey we think they look great – and no wastage. The quilt front and back were made by the authors and longarm quilted by The Quilt Room.

Cloudburst

For this striking quilt we chose one of the colourful ranges by Bonnie & Camille and mixed it with the fabulous Grunge Basics in grey from Moda. The tilted blocks give the quilt a great sense of movement and the colours would suit any modern decor. It is a quick and easy quilt to piece and the excess fabric from the pieced strip units worked perfectly for the quilt back. In the end we couldn't decide exactly which side of the quilt we preferred!

It looks as though you need a lot of background fabric for the quilt top but this is also used on the pieced quilt back. In fact, you only need an additional 2¼yd (2m) of background fabric and you have sufficient for your quilt back.

Vital Statistics

Quilt size: 68in x 68in

Block size: 9in

Number of blocks: 36

Setting: 6 x 6 blocks

Requirements
For quilt top:
- One jelly roll **OR** forty assorted 2½in strips cut across the width of the fabric
- Background fabric 6yd (5.75m)
- 9½in quilting square (optional)
- Binding fabric ½yd (0.5m)

For pieced quilt back:
- Backing fabric 2¼yd (2m)
- Thirty-six excess rectangles from quilt top, each about 6½in x 16in

Cloudburst Quilt

Preparation

Sorting the jelly roll strips:
- Choose thirty-six jelly roll strips for the blocks.
- Choose four jelly roll strips for the sashing squares.

Cutting the jelly roll strips:
- Take the four jelly roll strips allocated for the sashing squares and cut into forty-nine 2½in squares.
- Leave the remaining thirty-six strips uncut.

Cutting the background fabric:
- Cut thirty-six 4½in strips across the width of the fabric.
- Cut twenty-one 2½in strips across the width of the fabric and subcut each strip into four rectangles 2½in x 9½in to make eighty-four sashing strips.

Cutting the binding fabric:
- From the binding fabric cut seven 2½in wide strips across the width of the fabric.

Making the Quilt

Making a block

1 Sew one 2½in jelly roll strip to one 4½in background strip. Press towards the background fabric as shown.

2 Cut the strip into four 6½in squares. Set the remainder of the strip (approximately 6½in x 16in) aside for the pieced quilt back.

6½in square

3 Rotate the squares as shown and sew them together, pinning at the centre intersection to ensure a perfect match. Press the seams in the directions shown.

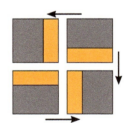

4 Place a 9½in quilting square on the sewn squares and tilt it as shown (see Tip overleaf). You can change the angle of tilt if you like as this will only enhance the look of your quilt. Cut around the square to form one block. The excess is spare but we saved ours, as we are sure we can use it in another project!

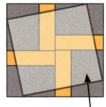

9½in quilting square

5 Repeat this process with all thirty-six jelly roll strips allocated for the blocks and thirty-six 4½in background strips to make a total of thirty-six blocks.

Make 36

Tip

If you don't have a 9½in quilting square you can make a temporary one from cardboard or clear plastic – just make sure it *is* 9½in square and right-angled. Don't use your cutter against the edge of this template as it won't be strong enough to be safe, just mark the shape with a pencil and then use a normal quilter's ruler to cut along the marked lines.

Adding the sashing

6 Sew six blocks together with a sashing strip in between and at both ends to make one row. Press towards the sashing strips. Repeat to make six rows.

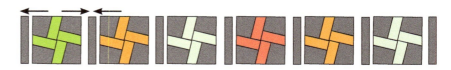

7 Sew six sashing strips together with a sashing square in between and at both ends to make one sashing row. Press towards the sashing strips. Repeat to make seven sashing rows.

8 Sew one sashing row to the top and bottom of the first row, pinning at every seam intersection for a perfect match.

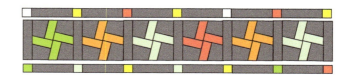

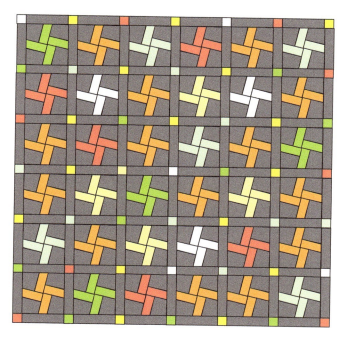

9 Continue sewing the six rows together with the seven sashing rows in between and at the top and bottom as shown. Press the completed quilt top.

Quilting and finishing

10 You can now make a quilt sandwich as normal with your wadding and backing fabric, ready for quilting. Alternatively, you could piece the back of the quilt as we did by referring to the instructions that follow.

11 After quilting, sew the seven binding strips into a continuous length and bind the quilt to finish.

After the backing was made our quilt was longarm quilted using a modern quilting design that has become a firm favourite – simple curved lines that flow in and out.

Making a Pieced Quilt Back

Cutting the backing fabric

1 Cut the following strips *lengthways* down the fabric (these will be trimmed to size later).
- Two strips 11½in wide, which will measure approximately 11½in x 76½in.
- Two strips 7½in wide, which will measure approximately 7½in x 76½in.

Assembling the backing

2 Sew the thirty-six excess rectangles (each approximately 6½in x 16in), into four rows of nine rectangles each.

3 Sew the rows together, rotating the second and fourth rows 180 degrees as shown in the diagram.

4 Determine the horizontal measurement from side to side across the centre of the quilt back and trim the 11½in wide backing strips to this measurement. Sew to the top and bottom of the quilt back and press.

5 Determine the vertical measurement from top to bottom through the centre of the quilt back and trim the 7½in wide strips to this measurement. Sew to the sides of the quilt back and press. Your quilt back can now be used to finish your quilt.

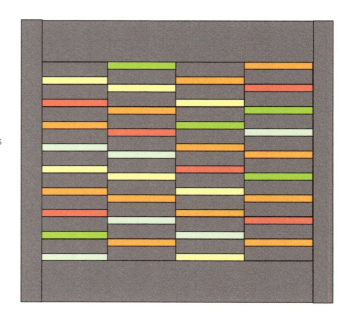

In this photograph of our quilt back you can see that the top and bottom of our quilt back are pieced strips. This was because we ran out of backing fabric! Did we panic – not a bit! – we just grabbed an assortment of strips to make up the size. The Requirements list gives sufficient fabric to make a plain, un-pieced border. The quilt front and back were made by the authors and longarm quilted by The Quilt Room.

Hexagon Star

There are some quilts that just make you smile and this is one of them. We just love this vibrant star set against a dramatic black background. The colours are bright and joyful and create a distinctly modern look. Although the design looks complex the pieces fell into place very easily.

We had twelve strips left over for our quilt back and again they just seemed to know where they should go. We hadn't planned to have four strips left over in three colourways but it was obviously meant to be! Making our three pyramids in three different colours worked brilliantly, but I'm sure they would work just as well in random colourways. Different placement of the pyramids would also ring the changes.

Vital Statistics

Quilt size: 62in x 76in

Block size: 8in triangles

Number of blocks: 48 60-degree triangles

Setting: 7 hexagons plus star points

Requirements

For quilt top:
- One jelly roll **OR** forty assorted 2½in strips cut across the width of the fabric
- Background fabric 3yd (2.75m)
- Binding fabric ½yd (50cm)
- 60-degree triangle ruler that will measure 8½in triangles

For pieced quilt back:
- Backing fabric 4¾yd (4.5m)
- Twelve spare strips from the jelly roll

Hexagon Star Quilt

Preparation

Sorting the jelly roll strips:
From your jelly roll choose the following.
- Seven Colour 1 dark strips (red).
- Seven Colour 2 medium strips (aqua/blue).
- Seven Colour 3 medium/light strips (green).
- Seven Colour 4 light strips (yellow/orange).

Cutting the background fabric:
- Cut four 8½in wide strips *across the width of the fabric*. Subcut each of these into one 8½in x 27½in rectangle and one 8½in x 9½in rectangle. You need four 8½in x 27½in rectangles and four 8½in x 9½in rectangles in total.
- Refold the remainder of the background fabric and cut the following *lengthways* down the fabric.
  - Two 6½in x length of fabric (approximately 65in).
  - Three 8½in x length of fabric. Subcut these as follows: one strip into four rectangles 8½in x 14in and two strips into four rectangles 8½in x 32in.
- Take two of the four 8½in x 9½in rectangles and using the 60-degree triangle as a guide cut a 60-degree angle on the right-hand side as shown.
- Take the remaining two 8½in x 9½in rectangles and using the 60-degree triangle as a guide cut a 60-degree angle on the left-hand side as shown.

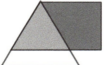

- Repeat with the four 8½in x 14in rectangles, the four 8½in x 27½in rectangles and the four 8½in x 32in rectangles, ensuring you cut two of each with the 60-degree angle on the *right* and two with the 60-degree angle on the *left*.

Cutting the binding fabric:
- Cut seven strips 2½in wide across the width of the fabric.

Making the Quilt

Making hexagon A

1. Take one strip each of Colours 1, 2, 3 and 4 and sew them together to form a strip unit as shown. Press the seams towards the darker fabric. Repeat to make seven strip units.

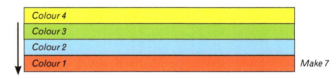

Make 7

2. Take one strip unit and place it on the cutting mat *with the dark Colour 1 strip on the bottom* as shown. Place the 60-degree triangle on the left-hand side of the strip unit, aligning the 8½in line of the triangle with the bottom of the strip unit and the cut-off top of the triangle with the top of the strip unit. Cut your first triangle.

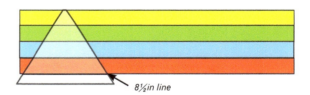

8½in line

3 Rotate the triangle ruler 180 degrees and cut the second triangle. Continue in this way to the end of the strip to cut seven triangles.

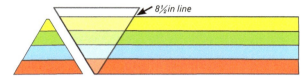

8½in line

4 You will now have four triangles with a Colour 1 base and three triangles with a Colour 4 base. Keep the seven triangles together in one pile as these will form one of the A hexagons. Repeat with three more of the strip units, keeping Colour 1 on the bottom of the strip unit.

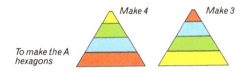

Make 4   Make 3

To make the A hexagons

Making hexagon B

5 Repeat this process with the remaining three strip units, but this time with the **dark Colour 1 strip on the top**.

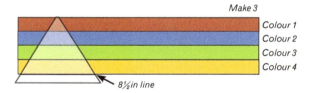

Make 3

Colour 1
Colour 2
Colour 3
Colour 4

8½in line

6 Keep the seven triangles from each strip unit together in one pile. These piles will have four triangles with Colour 4 on the base and three triangles with Colour 1 on the base. These will make the B hexagons.

Make 4   Make 3

To make the B hexagons

Assembling the hexagons

7 Select one pile of A hexagons to be the centre hexagon and lay out six triangles to form a hexagon, alternating the segments. The seventh triangle from this pile will not be needed. Do not sew anything together yet.

Centre hexagon

8 Lay out the remaining hexagons as shown in the diagram and use the seventh triangle from each pile to form the star points. Do not sew anything together yet but double check that everything is in the correct place. Now sew the triangles into eight horizontal rows, pinning at every seam intersection to ensure a perfect match.

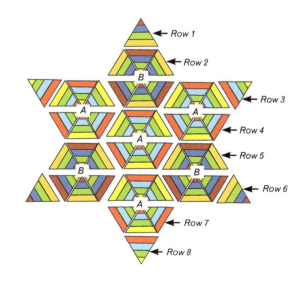

Row 1
Row 2
B
A   Row 3
A   A
A   Row 4
A   Row 5
B   B
Row 6
A   Row 7
Row 8

Adding the background

9 Place the background inserts at the end of each row as shown in the diagram and sew the rows together, pinning at every seam intersection to ensure a perfect match.

8½in x 32in

8½in x 27½in

8½in x 9½in

8½in x 14in

8½in x 14in

8½in x 9½in

8½in x 27½in

8½in x 32in

10 Sew the 6½in background strips to the top and bottom to complete the quilt top.

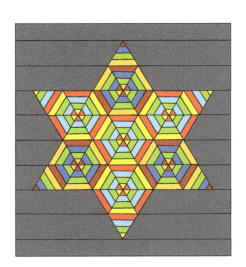

Quilting and finishing

11 You can now make a quilt sandwich as normal with your wadding (batting) and backing fabric, ready for quilting. Alternatively, you could piece the back of the quilt as we did by referring to the instructions that follow.

Tip

If you don't want a pieced back you could use a single fabric for the backing, but remember to make it larger than your quilt front, at least 4in larger on all sides.

12 After quilting, sew the seven binding strips into one length and bind the quilt to finish.

We chose a simple circle design and started the quilting small and dense at the top of the quilt and then increased the size of the circles by 30 per cent in each row. We used a pale lime green quilting thread to accentuate the quilting pattern and this colour worked especially well with the yellow fabric on the quilt back.

Making a Pieced Quilt Back

Cutting the backing fabric

1 Cut two 8½in strips across the width of the fabric. Using the 60-degree triangle, as shown, cut nine triangles.

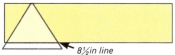

2 Cut six 24½in strips across the width of the fabric. Take three of these strips and cut a 60-degree angle on the left-hand side as shown. This can be done by using the 60-degree triangle and a long quilting ruler to extend the line.

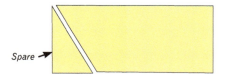

Spare →

3 Take three strips and cut a 60-degree angle on the right-hand side as shown. Measure 16½in from the left-hand side and trim to size.

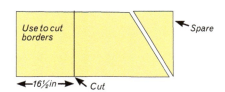

Use to cut borders

← Spare

←16½in→ ↘ Cut

4 Cut the 16½in x 24½in excess rectangles into 4in x 24½in strips. Sew together in a continuous length and use for the top and bottom borders.

Assembling the backing

5 Sew the twelve jelly roll strips into three strip units using four strips in each. We put ours into different colourways (blue, red and green). Using the 60-degree triangle ruler, cut six triangles from each strip unit.

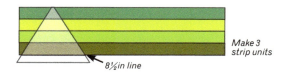

Make 3 strip units
8½in line

6 Sew six jelly roll triangles and three backing triangles together, to form a larger triangle as shown. Repeat to make three large triangles.

7 Sew the backing fabric pieces to the large triangles to make three rows.

8 Sew the rows together and then add the top and bottom borders to complete the quilt back.

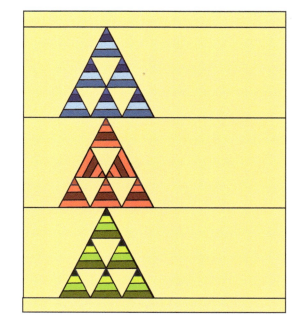

The triangles on the quilt back are the same as those on the quilt front and are made in exactly the same way, but here we have sewn them into three pyramids, alternating them with triangles from the solid yellow backing fabric. We chose lime green circles for our quilting, mainly with the quilt top in mind, but we think the quilting looks stunning against our solid yellow backing. The quilt front and back were made by the authors and longarm quilted by The Quilt Room.

Basket Weave

Big, bold and wonderfully modern, this quilt really shows what you can achieve with a few strips and an octagon! You need an octagon shape, which you can either draw yourself or photocopy and enlarge the template we've given. Once you realise how great the octagon shape is we know you'll be temped to use it a lot more! For this quilt we used a 90-degree triangle (see Suppliers). Any 90-degree triangle can be used, as long as it measures at least 6½in from the top of the triangle to the base line.

We used the offcuts from this quilt to make some nine-patch blocks for a small lap quilt, but you could use them to make a pieced quilt back instead. Your choices are endless!

Vital Statistics

Quilt size: 70in x 70in

Block size: 20½in

Number of blocks: 9

Setting: 3 x 3 blocks plus 2in sashing

Requirements
For quilt top:
- One jelly roll **OR** forty assorted 2½in strips cut across the width of the fabric
- Accent fabric 1⅜yd (1.25m)
- Background fabric 2¼yd (2.10m)
- Binding fabric ½yd (50cm)
- 90-degree triangle ruler, at least 6½in from top to bottom

For quilt back:
- Backing fabric 4½yd (4m) for an unpieced quilt back (we used our excess jelly roll strips to make a nine-patch lap quilt) **OR** 3½yd (3.25m) for a pieced quilt back

Basket Weave Quilt

Preparation

Sorting the jelly roll strips:
• Pair up your jelly roll strips into pairs of similar colouring. Two pairs of strips plus two accent fabric strips will make one block. We found a jelly roll that had a number of duplicate strips, which was perfect. You need eighteen pairs of jelly roll strips.

• Choose one strip for the sashing squares.

• Three strips are spare.

Cutting the jelly roll strips:
• Cut the strip allocated for the sashing squares into sixteen 2½in squares.

• Leave the other jelly roll strips uncut.

Cutting the accent fabric:
• Cut eighteen 2½in wide strips across the width of the fabric.

Cutting the background fabric:
• Cut three 9in strips across the width of the fabric. Using a 3¾in octagon template (given here), cut three 3¾in octagons from each strip, making a total of nine octagons. Note: This 3¾in measurement refers to the measurement of each of the eight sides of the octagon.

• Cut three 7in strips across the width of the fabric. Subcut each strip into six 7in squares. Cut each of the eighteen squares in half diagonally to create thirty-six corner triangles.

• Cut twelve 2½in strips across the width of the fabric. Subcut each strip into two rectangles 2½in x 21in. These are for the sashing strips and you need twenty-four sashing rectangles in total.

Cutting the binding fabric:
• Cut seven 2½in wide strips across the width of the fabric.

Making the octagon template:
The template can be made in either of the following ways:

A) Enlarge the octagon shape supplied here – it is shown at quarter size so enlarge it by 400% on a photocopier. Do check your full size template is accurate – each side should measure exactly 3¾in.

B) Draw your own template as follows.
• Using your quilting ruler, draw a line that measures 3¾in.

• Line up the 45-degree marker on your quilting ruler on this line and draw the next side of the octagon at an angle of 45 degrees.

• Measure and mark that line at 3¾in. Continue in this way to draw each side at 45 degrees.

• Once you have drawn the octagon double check that each side measures 3¾in before using it as a template to cut out the octagons from fabric.

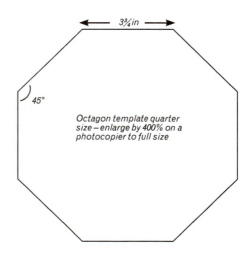

3¾in

45°

Octagon template quarter size – enlarge by 400% on a photocopier to full size

Making the Quilt

Making a block

1 Choose two pairs of jelly roll strips that are different colours, plus two accent strips.

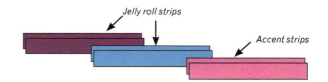

Jelly roll strips

Accent strips

2 Sew two strip units together as shown, making sure the strips are kept in the same order for both strip units. Ensure the accent fabric is placed at the top. You do not want to have the accent strip in the centre. Press seams in one direction.

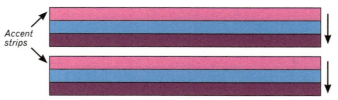

Accent strips

3 Place the 90-degree triangle on the strip unit, as far to the left as possible, lining up the 6½in line along the bottom of the strip unit and the cut-off top of the triangle along the top. Cut the first triangle.

6½in line

4 Rotate the triangle 180 degrees, placing the 6½in strip line along the top edge of the strip unit and the cut-off top of the triangle on the bottom. Cut a second triangle. Repeat to cut four triangles in total. Note: the remainder of the strip unit, which measures approximately 7½in, is spare. To use this in a lap quilt, or as a pieced quilt back, refer to the instructions at the end of the pattern.

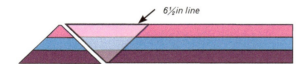

6½in line

5 You should now have two different types of triangles – one with the accent fabric as the small triangle at the top and the other with the accent fabric as the large strip at the bottom. You should have four each of these triangles.

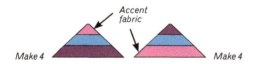

Accent fabric

Make 4   Make 4

6 Take a triangle with the accent fabric at the top and, with right sides together, sew it to one side of the octagon, but sew only half of the seam (a partial seam), as shown. Note that the corner of your triangle will overlap the octagon as shown.

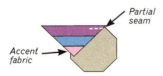

Partial seam

Accent fabric

7 Gently press open. Remember you are dealing with bias edges so handle carefully and do not use steam. You will see that the triangle you have sewn and the next octagon side now have a straight edge.

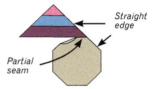

Straight edge

Partial seam

8 Take a triangle with the accent fabric at the bottom and, with right sides together, sew it to the first triangle as shown. Press open (no steam), handling bias edges carefully.

9 Now take a triangle with the accent fabric at the top and, with right sides together, sew it to the second triangle as shown. Press open.

10 Continue in this way to sew the triangles all round the octagon. When you have sewn the eighth triangle you can then complete the first partial seam.

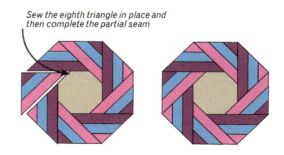

Sew the eighth triangle in place and then complete the partial seam

11 Sew a corner triangle to each corner to complete the block. Press the block, pressing seams outwards. Trim the corners to square up the block if necessary. Your block should measure 21in square.

12 Repeat the process described in steps 1–11 to make nine blocks in total.

Adding the sashing strips

13 Sew a 2½in x 21in sashing strip to the left-hand and right-hand side of one block and to the right-hand side of two blocks, as shown. Press towards the sashing.

14 Sew three sashing strips with four 2½in sashing squares together as shown to make one horizontal sashing strip. Repeat to make four of these.

15 Sew a horizontal sashing strip to the top and bottom of the first row and to the bottom of the other two rows, pinning at every seam intersection to ensure a perfect match and easing if necessary. Now sew the rows together.

Quilting and finishing

16 You can now make a quilt sandwich as normal with your wadding (batting) and backing fabric, ready for quilting. Alternatively, make a pieced backing (see overleaf).

17 After quilting, sew the binding strips into one continuous length and bind the quilt to finish.

For the quilting, we chose a very popular dragonfly pattern and to make them really stand out against the background fabric we used a colourful variegated thread.

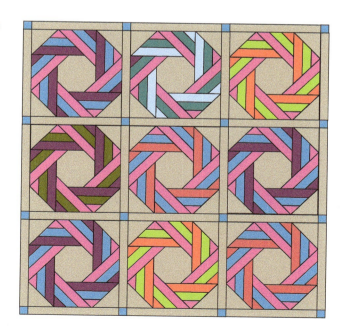

Making a Pieced Quilt Back

The excess strips from our Basket Weave Quilt were perfect for making a nine-patch design. You can either use these blocks to make a pieced back for your quilt or use them in a small lap quilt as we did. To make a lap quilt 39in x 51in with 6½in square blocks, follow the instructions below. To make a pieced back, follow the same instructions but add an additional border all round, to bring the piecing up to 78in square for your Basket Weave Quilt.

Cutting fabrics if making a lap quilt

1 Cut three 6½in strips across the width of the additional fabric and subcut these strips into seventeen 6½in squares.

2 You will need 1¼yd (1.10m) of additional fabric for the border. Cut four 5in strips across the width of the fabric for the borders.

Cutting fabrics if making a pieced backing

1 Cut three 6½in strips across the width of the additional fabric and subcut these strips into seventeen 6½in squares.

2 If making as a backing you will need a wider border. You will need 3½yd (3.25m) of additional fabric for this. Cut two pieces 24½in wide across the width of the fabric for the side borders. Cut four pieces 18½in wide across the width of the fabric for the top and bottom borders. Join the strips in pairs so they are long enough.

Making the nine-patch blocks

3 Gather up the excess fabric from the strip units made for the Basket Weave quilt and cut into 2½in segments. You also have three spare jelly roll strips that could be sewn together into a strip unit and then cut up into 2½in segments.

4 Mix up the segments and sew three segments together to make a nine-patch block. Make eighteen nine-patch blocks in total.

Make 18

Assembling the quilt

5 Lay out the blocks, alternating a nine-patch block with a 6½in square, as shown. When you are happy with the layout sew the blocks into rows and then sew the rows together. If you always press your seams towards the background square your seams will nest together nicely when sewing the rows together.

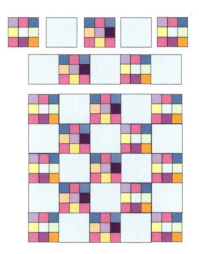

6 Sew on the border strips, sewing the side borders on first and pressing seams outwards. Use the narrower borders for the lap quilt or the wider borders for the backing. Sew on the top and bottom borders to complete your quilt top.

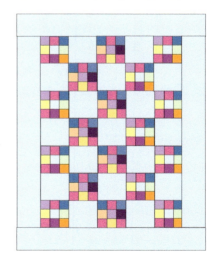

7 If making the lap quilt, make a quilt sandwich as normal with wadding (batting) and backing, ready for quilting. Bind the lap quilt to finish.

The leftover segments from the Basket Weave quilt can be used to make a lap quilt, as shown here, or a wider border can be added to make the design big enough for a pieced backing to the Basket Weave quilt. The quilt front and back were made by the authors and longarm quilted by The Quilt Room.

Spangles

This exciting contemporary quilt, with its colourful geometric layout, would update any room. We've given precise instructions for the blocks but don't feel inhibited – you can construct your blocks any way, as long as the squares are 6½in or 12½in and the rectangles are 12½in x 18½in. You could make the quilt top using just one jelly roll (although it's a bit tight) but we've allowed an extra ½yd (50cm) each of two coordinating solids. This extra fabric can be cut into 1½in and 2½in strips and used when you're stuck for a jelly roll strip to use.

Some of our 2½in jelly roll strips were trimmed down to 1½in wide to make our Log Cabin blocks and the 1in wide offcuts were perfect for the 'bubbles' on the quilt back. We used a colourful range called Wishes from Sweetwater by Moda and added a coordinating red and green solid.

Vital Statistics

Quilt size: 56in x 62in

Block size: 6in and 12in squares and 12in x 18in rectangles

Number of blocks: twenty-four 6in blocks, seven 12in blocks, two 12in x 18in rectangular blocks and four strippy 6in x 12in rectangles

Setting: random with 1in inner border and 3in outer border

Requirements
For quilt top:
- One jelly roll **OR** forty assorted 2½in strips cut across the width of the fabric
- Coordinating green solid ½yd (50cm)
- Coordinating red solid ½yd (50cm)
- Inner border fabric ⅜yd (25cm)
- Outer border fabric ¾yd (60cm)
- Binding fabric ½yd (50cm)

For pieced quilt back:
- Backing fabric 3yd (2.75m)
- Offcuts from quilt top

Spangles Quilt

Preparation

Sorting the strips:
There is no initial sorting of fabric as we selected our strips as we were cutting and sewing the blocks.

Cutting the coordinating solid fabrics:
• Cut four 1½in strips and four 2½in across the width of the fabric to use with the jelly roll strips to make the blocks. You can cut more when required.

Cutting the inner border fabric:
• Cut six strips 1½in wide across the width of the fabric.

Cutting the outer border fabric:
• Cut six strips 3½in wide across the width of the fabric.

Cutting the binding fabric:
• Cut six strips 2½in wide across the width of the fabric.

Making the Quilt

Making the block centres
1 Choose one 2½in strip from one of the coordinating solids and cut sixteen 2½in squares for the block centres. You need thirty-one 2½in centre squares in total and two 2½in x 6½in centre rectangles. We cut the remaining block centres from offcuts from the jelly roll strips once we got started on our blocks.

Making block A
2 Half a jelly roll strip will make one block. Cut the half strip as follows.
• Two 2½in squares.
• Two 2½in x 6½in rectangles.

3 Sew the two 2½in squares to a centre square and press away from the centre. Sew the 2½in x 6½in rectangles to the top and bottom and press as shown. Repeat to make ten Block A using a variety of strips.

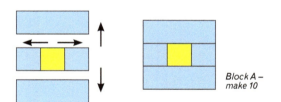

Block A – make 10

Making block B

 Half a jelly roll strip will make the inner round of one block. Trim a jelly roll strip to measure 1½in wide (or use a 1½in strip cut from the coordinating fabric) and cut as follows.
- Two 1½in x 2½in rectangles.
- Two 1½in x 4½in rectangles.

5 Sew the two 1½in x 2½in rectangles to a centre square and press away from the centre. Sew the 1½in x 4½in rectangles to the top and bottom and press as shown.

Tip

When making the blocks, substituting 1½in wide strips of the coordinating solids saves excess wastage from the jelly roll strips.

6 Three-quarters of a jelly roll strip will make the outer round of one block. Trim the jelly roll strip to measure 1½in wide (or use a 1½in strip cut from the coordinating fabric) and cut as follows.
- Two 1½in x 4½in rectangles.
- Two 1½in x 6½in rectangles.

7 Sew the rectangles on as shown and press. Repeat to make fourteen Block B, using a variety of strips. Set all spare strips aside for the strippy rectangles and quilt back.

Making block C

8 Half a jelly roll strip will make the inner round of one block. Cut as follows.
- Two 2½in squares.
- Two 2½in x 6½in rectangles.

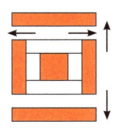

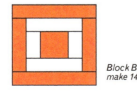

Block B – make 14

9 Sew the two 2½in squares to either side of a centre square and press. Sew the 2½in x 6½in rectangles to the top and bottom and press as shown.

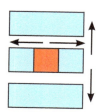

10 Half a jelly roll strip will make the middle round of one block. Trim to measure 1½in wide (or use a 1½in strip cut from the coordinating fabric) and cut as follows.
- Two 1½in x 6½in rectangles.
- Two 1½in x 8½in rectangles.

Sew the rectangles on as shown and press.

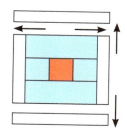

11 One jelly roll strip will make the outer round of one block. Cut the strips as follows.
- Two 2½in x 8½in rectangles.
- Two 2½in x 12½in rectangles.

Sew the rectangles on as shown and press. Repeat to make seven of Block C, using a variety of strips.

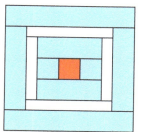

Block C – make 7

Making block D

12 One jelly roll strip will make the inner round of one block. Cut as follows.
- Two 2½in squares.
- Two 2½in x 10½in rectangles.

13 Sew the two 2½in squares to a 2½in x 6½in centre rectangle and press. Sew the 2½in x 10½in rectangles to the top and bottom and press as shown.

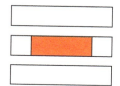

14 One jelly roll strip will make the second round of one block. Trim to measure 1½in wide (or use a 1½in strip cut from the coordinating fabric) and cut as follows.
- Two 1½in x 6½in rectangles.
- Two 1½in x 12½in rectangles.

Sew the rectangles on and press.

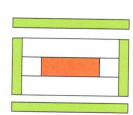

15 One and a half jelly roll strips will make the third round of one block. Cut as follows.
- Two 2½in x 8½in rectangles.
- Two 2½in x 16½in rectangles.

Sew the rectangles on as shown and press.

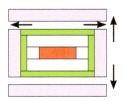

16 One 1½in wide strip will make the two rectangles for the sides. Cut two strips 1½in x 12½in. Sew to the sides of the block. Repeat to make two Block D using a variety of strips.

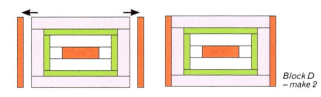

Block D – make 2

Making block E

17 Choose a selection of offcuts and trim them to measure 12½in long. Sew them together to make a rectangle 6½in x 12½in. This can be as scrappy as you like. Repeat to make four of Block E.

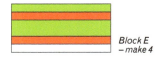

Block E – make 4

Assembling the quilt

18 Lay out your blocks referring to the piecing diagram. When you are happy with the layout, sew the 6in blocks together first and then sew the remaining blocks together as shown in the diagram.

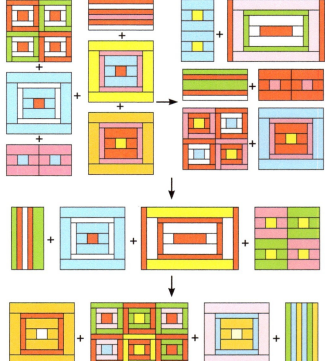

Adding the borders

19 The quilt has a narrow inner border and a wider outer border. For the inner border, sew the six 1½in inner border strips into a continuous length. Determine the vertical measurement from top to bottom through the centre of your quilt top, and cut two side borders to this measurement. Pin and sew to the quilt. Press the seams.

20 Determine the horizontal measurement from side to side across the centre of the quilt top. Cut two borders to this measurement and sew to the top and bottom of the quilt. Press the seams.

21 Repeat this process to add the outer border, using the six 3½in border strips. Sew to the quilt the same way.

Quilting and finishing

22 You can now make a quilt sandwich as normal with your wadding (batting) and backing fabric, ready for quilting. Alternatively, you could piece the back of the quilt as we did by referring to the instructions that follow.

23 After quilting, sew the six binding strips into a continuous length and bind the quilt to finish.

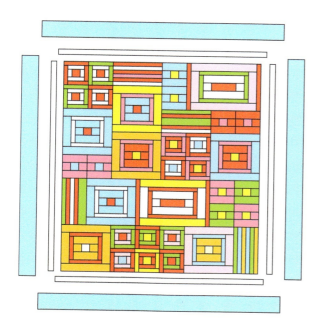

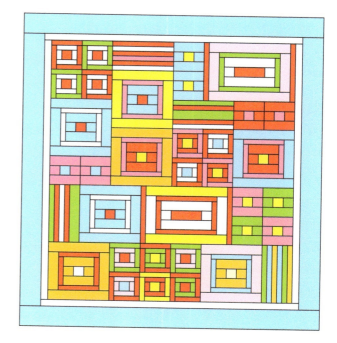

We wanted a circular quilting pattern to complement the squares and rectangles in our quilt top and we chose an edge-to-edge design of interlocking circles, which created a secondary pattern similar to Japanese folded patchwork.

Making a Pieced Quilt Back

Sorting the jelly roll strips

1 You will have lots of excess strips in varying widths left over from the jelly roll strips used to make the quilt front, plus you will have some coordinating fabric left, which can be cut into strips if needed.

Cutting the backing fabric

2 Cut three lengths of 35in and then subcut one in half to create two rectangles 35in x 21in. You will have two rectangles 35in x 42in and two rectangles 35in x 21in.

Assembling the backing

3 Sew strips into rectangles large enough to create circles using a variety of different plate sizes as templates – approximately 10in, 8in and 6in diameter.

4 Using the plates as templates, cut out circles from the sewn rectangle strips *1in larger all round*. Sew around the outer edge of the circle to stabilize the strips.

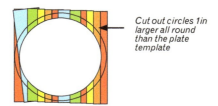

Cut out circles 1in larger all round than the plate template

5 Decide where you want to place your circles on the quilt back and, using the plates as templates, mark the circles on your pieces of background fabric. Cut out the circles exactly on the marked line. This means that the circles on your backing fabric wil be 1in smaller than your pieced circles.

Pin all round

6 Pin the strippy circles in place securely *under* the circular shapes cut out of the backing fabric, pinning in place all round. Work the reverse appliqué by turning under and pinning the raw edge of the backing fabric around the circle. Hand sew in place.

7 Sew the background rectangles together, as shown, to complete the quilt back.

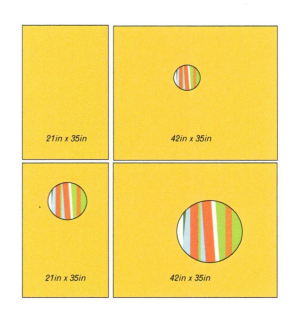

21in x 35in
42in x 35in
21in x 35in
42in x 35in

With a little bit of reverse appliqué you can create a stunning, minimalist quilt from the smallest of leftovers. Our original plan was to have lots of small bubbles but in the end we made just three in different sizes and liked the simplicity of this. Lots of smaller ones would have taken a lot longer – maybe that's why we decided on just three! The quilt front and back were made by the authors and longarm quilted by *The Quilt Room*.

Diamond Drops

The jelly roll we used was Little Black Dress 2 from Moda, which had an equal number of very light strips and dark strips. We picked out twenty dark strips to make our diamond drops and set the diamonds against a nearly solid tan fabric to create a stunning contemporary quilt design.

This left us with twenty light strips to make our quilt back and we chose a solid cream for the background, which created a much quieter but sophisticated quilt. Looking at the photo of our quilt back, you will notice that the quilting is a different design from the one on the quilt top – we can't keep anything secret! We decided we loved the quilt back so much it needed to be a quilt in its own right. We ended up with two separate quilts on this occasion and that is a choice you have with any of our pieced quilt backs.

Vital Statistics

Quilt size: 64in x 76in

Setting: 7 rows of 9 diamonds, plus 2in border

Requirements

For quilt top:
• One jelly roll **OR** forty assorted 2½in strips cut across the width of the fabric

• Background fabric 4yd (3.75m)

• Binding fabric ½yd (50cm)

• 60-degree triangle ruler that measures triangles up to 8½in

For pieced quilt back:
• Twenty spare jelly roll strips

• Backing fabric 4yd (3.75m)

Diamond Drops Quilt

Preparation

Sorting the jelly roll strips:
• Choose twenty dark jelly roll strips for the diamonds.

Cutting the background fabric:
• Cut twenty-nine 4½in strips across the width of the fabric.
• Cut four 2½in wide strips across the width of the fabric and set aside for the top and bottom borders.

Cutting the binding fabric:
• Cut seven 2½in wide strips across the width of the fabric.

Making the Quilt

Making the strip-pieced triangles

1 Pair up the twenty jelly roll strips and sew each pair together to make ten strip units. Press as shown.

Make 10

2 Lay the 60-degree triangle on the strip unit as shown, lining up the 4½in line of the ruler with the bottom edge of the strip unit. Cut the first triangle.

4½in line

3 Rotate the ruler 180 degrees and cut the second triangle. Continue along the strip cutting thirteen triangles.

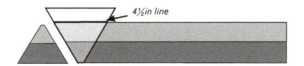

4½in line

4 Repeat with all ten strip units to make a total of 130 triangles. You need 126, so four are spare.

Make 126 triangles

5 Take a 4½in background strip and place the 60-degree triangle on the strip as shown with the 3½in line along the top and the 8in line along the bottom. Mark these lines on your 60-degree triangle with masking tape (see Tip). Cut the first half-hexagon. Rotate the triangle and continue to cut five half-hexagons from one strip.

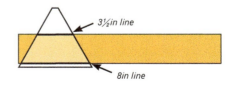

3½in line

8in line

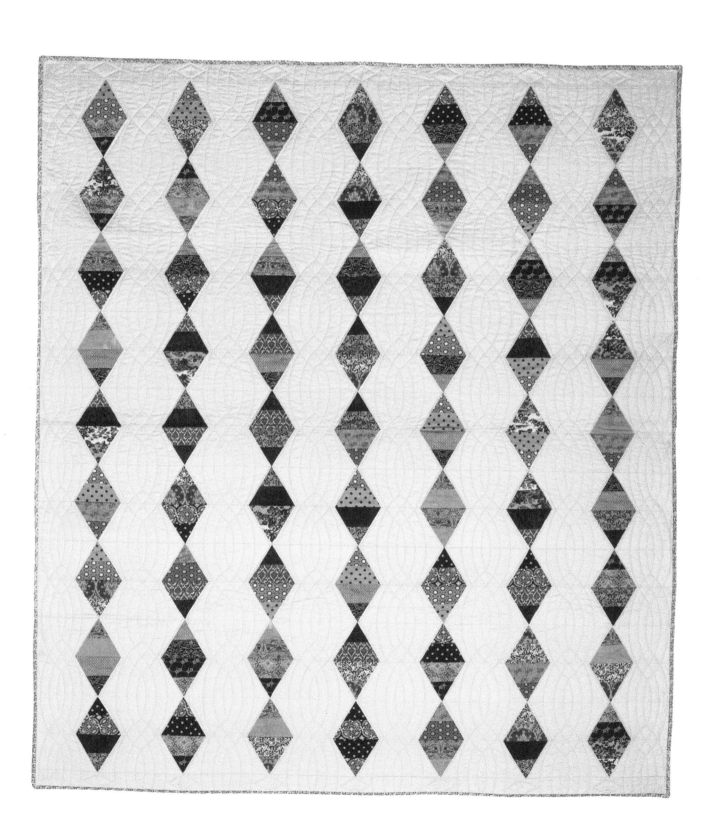

Tip

Using masking tape to mark the lines on your triangle ruler will help to ensure that you always line up on the correct markings.

6 Repeat with all twenty-nine 4½in background strips to make a total of 145 background half-hexagons. You need 144, so one is spare.

Make 144 half-hexagons

Assembling the quilt rows

7 Take a 60-degree jelly roll triangle and, with right sides together, sew it to a background half-hexagon as shown. When joining strips with angled cuts there will be an overlap at each end, so check for accuracy.

8 Open and press towards the half-hexagon. Repeat to make seven units like this.

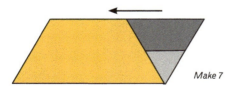

Make 7

9 Sew the seven units together to make one row and sew on an extra half-hexagon to complete the row. Repeat to make two rows.

Make 2 rows

10 Rotate one row 180 degrees and sew together, pinning at every seam intersection to ensure a perfect match. Press the seam. These two rows create the diamonds.

11 Repeat steps 7–10 eight more times to create nine diamond rows in total.

12 Lay out the nine diamond rows and when you are happy with the layout, sew the rows together, pinning at every seam intersection to ensure a perfect match.

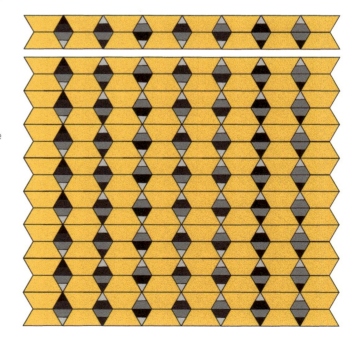

13 Using a long quilting ruler, straighten the side edges of your quilt top.

Adding the border

14 Determine the horizontal measurement from side to side across the centre of the quilt top. Sew two border strips together and trim to this measurement. Sew to the top of the quilt. Repeat with the remaining two border strips and sew to the bottom of the quilt. Your quilt top is now ready for quilting.

Quilting and finishing

15 You can now make a quilt sandwich as normal with your wadding (batting) and backing fabric, ready for quilting. Alternatively, you could piece the back of the quilt as we did by referring to the instructions that follow.

16 Sew the seven binding strips into a continuous length and bind the quilt to finish.

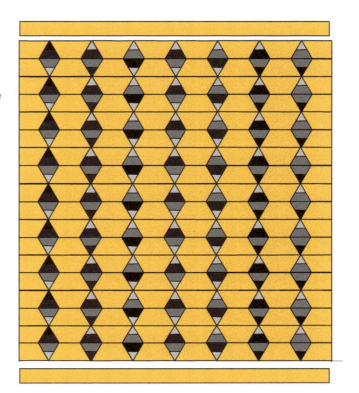

We quilted around our diamonds to accentuate them and then chose a simple cable design to quilt vertically in between.

Making a Pieced Quilt Back

The pieced back of our Diamond Drops Quilt actually became a separate quilt, so each quilt had its own wadding (batting) and backing fabric. If you also decide to make a separate quilt with the pieced back, the Diamond Drops Quilt will need unpieced backing fabric of 4yd (3.75m). Follow the instructions below for a pieced quilt back, and then you can decide.

Cutting the backing fabric

1. Cut sixteen 4½in strips across the width of the fabric. Re-fold the remaining fabric lengthways (approximately 72in) and cut two strips 8in wide and two strips 13in wide. These will be trimmed to size later.

Sewing the rows together

2. Pair up the twenty jelly roll strips and sew into ten strip units. Using the marked 60-degree triangle used for the quilt top cut each strip unit into five half-hexagons (a total of fifty).

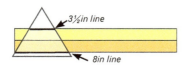

3. Repeat with the sixteen 4½in background strips to make a total of 80 background half-hexagons. You need 76, so four are spare.

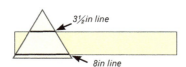

4. To create rows 1 and 2, sew five background half-hexagons together with four jelly roll half-hexagons as shown to make each row. Press towards the half-hexagons. Rotate one row 180 degrees and sew the two rows together, pinning at every seam intersection to ensure a perfect match. Repeat rows 1 and 2 four times.

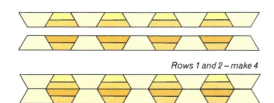

Rows 1 and 2 – make 4

5. To create rows 3 and 4, sew six background half-hexagons together with three jelly roll half-hexagons to make each row. Press towards the background half-hexagons. Rotate one row 180 degrees and sew the two rows together, pinning at every seam intersection. Repeat rows 3 and 4 three times.

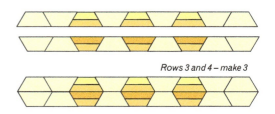

Rows 3 and 4 – make 3

Assembling the quilt back

6. Sew the rows together as shown, alternating rows 1 and 2 with rows 3 and 4, finishing with rows 1 and 2. Press the seams. Straighten the uneven side edges using a long quilting ruler.

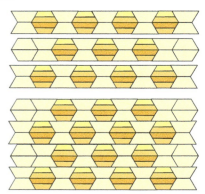

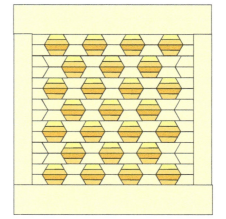

Adding the border

7. Measure vertically from top to bottom through the centre of the quilt back and trim the 8in wide side borders to size. Sew to the quilt back. Measure the quilt horizontally and repeat with the 13in top and bottom borders.

After choosing the twenty dark jelly roll strips for Diamond Drops, we made what was going to be the reverse of the quilt using the twenty light strips. We liked it so much we decided it had to become a quilt on its own. Don't forget that you can do this with any of the patterns in this book – you can have a double-sided quilt or you can make two quilts as we did – the choice is yours! The quilt front and back were made by the authors and longarm quilted by The Quilt Room.

Ocean Deep

This quilt has an excitingly modern look and we loved using this jelly roll, designed by Janet Clare from her first fabric range Hearty Good Wishes for Moda. Janet is based near us in the UK and often teaches in our shop. It was a perfect jelly roll to use as it had the right mix of lights to darks, which is needed to create the striking three-dimensional effect in our Ocean Deep quilt.

On the quilt back we couldn't resist trying out these colourways for the Hexagon Star pattern featured on a quilt described earlier in the book. We think it works really well and you definitely have a double-sided quilt here – it certainly would be very difficult to know which side to keep for best!

Vital Statistics

Quilt size: 66in x 80in

Block size: 8in 60-degree triangles

Number of blocks: 42

Setting: 4 vertical rows, plus 6in vertical sashing

Requirements

For quilt top:
- One jelly roll **OR** forty assorted 2½in strips cut across the width of the fabric
- Background fabric 3¼yd (3m)
- Binding fabric ⅝yd (60cm)
- 60-degree triangle ruler that will measure 8½in triangles

For pieced quilt back:
- Backing fabric 4½yd (4m)
- Sixteen spare jelly roll strips from jelly roll
- Four long ¼yd/m to cut extra jelly roll strips

Ocean Deep Quilt

Preparation

Sorting your jelly roll strips:
• Artistic licence can be used here but you do need to grade from dark to light to create the three-dimensional effect. From your jelly roll strips choose the following.

   – Six Colour 1 dark strips.
   – Six Colour 2 dark/medium strips.
   – Six Colour 3 medium strips.
   – Six Colour 4 light strips.

Cutting the background fabric:
• Cut four 8½in strips across the width of the fabric and subcut them as follows.

   – Two 8½in x 26in rectangles.
   – Two 8½in x 12½in rectangles.
   – Two 8½in x 24½in rectangles.
   – Two 8½in x 15½in rectangles.

• The remaining background fabric will measure at least 80in and can be trimmed to size later. Refold this *lengthways* and cut as follows.

   – Two 8½in wide strips for the borders.
   – Three 6½in wide strips for the sashing.

• Take the two 8½in x 26in rectangles and place them on your cutting mat *right side up* on top of each other, aligning the edges. Using the 60-degree triangle as a guide, cut a 60-degree angle on the right-hand side. Repeat with the two 8½in x 24½in rectangles and the two 8½in x 15½in rectangles.

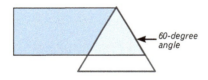

• Take the two 8½in x 12½in rectangles and with *both rectangles right side up* cut a 60-degree angle on the left-hand side, as shown.

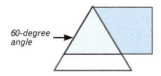

Cutting the binding fabric:
• Cut eight strips 2½in wide across the width of the fabric.

Making the Quilt

Making the triangle units

1 Take one strip each of Colours 1, 2, 3 and 4 and sew them together to form a strip unit as shown. Press the seams towards the darker fabric. Repeat to make six strip units.

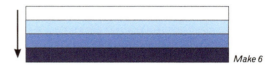

Make 6

2 Take one strip unit and place it on the cutting mat with the dark Colour 1 strip on the bottom as shown. Place the 60-degree triangle ruler on the left side of the strip unit, aligning the 8½in line of the triangle with the bottom of the strip unit and the cut-off top of the triangle with the top of the strip unit. Cut your first triangle.

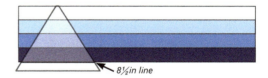

8½in line

3 Rotate the ruler 180 degrees and cut the second triangle. Continue to the end of the strip to cut seven triangles. You will have four with a dark base and three with a light base. Repeat this process with a second strip unit.

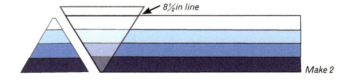

8½in line

Make 2

4 Rotate the remaining four strip units 180 degrees so the dark Colour 1 strip is now on the top and repeat the process to cut seven triangles from each strip unit. Each strip will give four with a light base and three with a dark base.

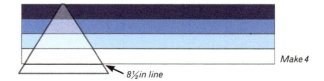

Make 4

8½in line

5 You will have twenty triangles with a dark Colour 1 base and twenty-two triangles with a light Colour 4 base.

Make 20

Make 22

Assembling the vertical rows

6 Choose ten triangles with a dark base and sew them into one vertical row. Press gently in the direction shown after sewing each one. This will make it easier to match up the triangles when sewing the triangles together.

Tip

When sewing the triangles together, remember that you are dealing with bias edges, so handle the fabric gently and when pressing do not use steam.

7 Sew an 8½in x 15½in background rectangle to the top and an 8½in x 26in background rectangle to the bottom of the vertical row. Repeat to make a total of two vertical rows of ten triangles with the dark fabric at the base.

Make 2 rows

8 Repeat to make two vertical rows of eleven triangles with the light fabric at the base and sew an 8½in x 24½in background rectangle to the top and an 8½in x 12½in background rectangle to the bottom.

Make 2 rows

9 Measure the vertical rows and trim the sashing and border strips to the same length. It is important that they all measure the same.

10 Sew the vertical rows together with a 6½in wide sashing strip in between, pinning and easing where necessary. Now sew on the two 8½in wide side borders.

Quilting and finishing

11 Your quilt top is now complete. You can make a quilt sandwich as normal with your wadding (batting) and backing fabric, ready for quilting. Alternatively, you could piece the back of the quilt as we did by referring to the instructions that follow.

12 Sew the eight binding strips into a continuous length and bind the quilt to finish.

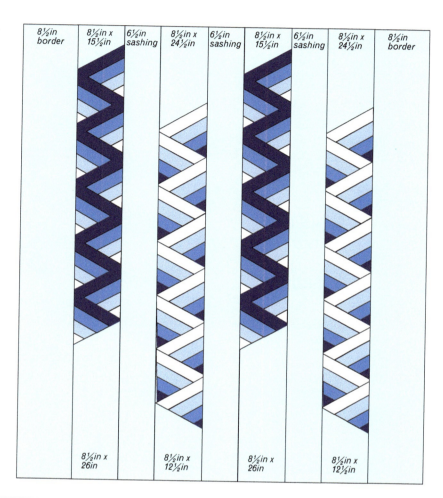

We chose a design called Modern Curves by Anita Shackleford as the perfect quilting complement for this quilt. Its wavy curves echoed the design of the fabrics and created a gorgeous nautical feel in the quilt. We used a neutral quilting thread that blended well.

Making a Pieced Quilt Back

We used the Hexagon Star pattern for the back of this quilt – please refer to that chapter for instructions on cutting and piecing the Hexagon Star pattern. You will need to add an extra border to create the correct size for this backing.

Cutting the four long quarters

1 Cut each of the long quarters into three 2½in strips across the width of the fabric to make twelve 2½in strips. These can be added to the sixteen spare jelly roll strips from the quilt top as twenty-eight are needed in total.

Cutting the backing fabric

2 Cut the following strips for the extra border of backing fabric required.

- Four 4in strips across the width of the fabric.

- Four 8in strips across the width of the fabric.

3 Cut the remaining backing fabric as noted in the Hexagon Star Quilt: Cutting the Backing Fabric.

Assembling the pieced backing

4 Follow steps 1–10 in the Hexagon Star chapter to create the hexagon star design.

5 Sew two 4in strips together. Repeat with the other two 4in strips. Determine the vertical measurement from top to bottom through the centre of your quilt back and trim the two side borders to this measurement. Pin and sew to the quilt back and press.

6 Sew two 8in strips together. Repeat with the other two 8in strips. Determine the horizontal measurement from side to side across the centre of the quilt back. Trim two borders to this measurement, sew to the top and bottom of the quilt back and then press. The quilt back is now ready to use.

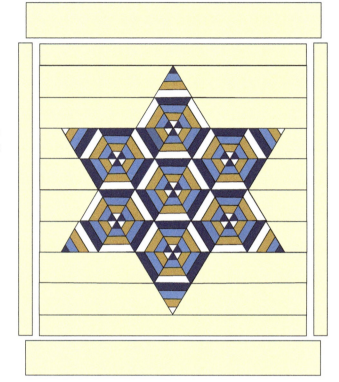

The reverse of the Ocean Deep quilt uses the Hexagon Star pattern. We loved the pattern in the bright colourful colours we used in the Hexagon Star quilt and it was just too tempting to see how it would look with more subdued colours. We certainly love the effect and hope you agree. The quilt front and back were made by the authors and longarm quilted by The Quilt Room.

Interlocking Chains

This striking quilt is quick to piece, but a bit like a jigsaw puzzle when you come to sew the blocks together. However, we've given clear diagrams, so all you need to do is follow them. The quilt looks impressive and is definitely worth the extra attention. Even though our chains are scrappy, it's very important to have two distinct colour groups so the interlocking circles are clearly seen. We used a great jelly roll called Winter Wonderland from Moda that had the perfect mix of reds and whites.

The back of the quilt features a really easy, traditional arrangement of sixteen-patch blocks alternating against a light grey solid.

Vital Statistics

Quilt size: 54in x 66in

Block size: 6in square

Number of blocks: 99

Setting: 9 blocks x 11 blocks

Requirements
For quilt top:
- One jelly roll **OR** forty assorted 2½in strips cut across the width of the fabric
- Background fabric 2½yd (2.25m)
- Binding fabric ½yd (50cm)

For pieced quilt back:
- Backing fabric 3yd (2.75m)
- Twelve spare jelly roll strips

Interlocking Chains Quilt

Preparation

Sorting the jelly roll strips:
You will need to be guided by what is in your jelly roll and artistic licence can be used but it is important to have two distinct colour groups. You need the following.
- Fifteen colour A (red) strips.
- Thirteen colour B (white) strips.

Cutting the colour A (red) jelly roll strips:
- Take four colour A strips and cut each strip into sixteen 2½in squares to make a total of sixty-four.
- Take eight colour A strips and cut each strip into eight 2½in x 4½in rectangles to make a total of sixty-four. You need fifty-eight, so six are spare.
- Take three colour A strips and cut each strip into six 2½in x 6½in rectangles to make a total of eighteen. You need fourteen, so four are spare.

Cutting the colour B (white) jelly roll strips:
- Take four colour B strips and cut each strip into sixteen 2½in squares to make a total of sixty-four.
- Take seven colour B strips and cut each strip into eight 2½in x 4½in rectangles to make a total of fifty-six.
- Take two colour B strips and cut each strip into six 2½in x 6½in rectangles to make a total of twelve. You need eight, so four are spare.

Cutting the background fabric:
- Cut ten 6½in strips across the width of the fabric. Subcut these into the following.
    - Fifty-five 6½in squares.
    - Four 4½in x 6½in rectangles.
- Cut two 4½in strips across the width of the fabric. Subcut these into the following.
    - Ten 4½in squares.
    - Eight 2½in x 4½in rectangles.
- Cut two 2½in strips across the width of the fabric. Subcut these into the following.
    - Twenty-two 2½in squares.

Cutting the binding fabric:
- Cut seven 2½in strips across the width of the fabric.

Making the Quilt

Making block A

1 Take a colour A 2½in x 4½in rectangle and, with right sides together, sew it halfway along a 2½in background square. Press open. This is a partial seam and will be completed after the last rectangle has been sewn on.

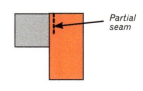

Partial seam

2 Sew a colour B 2½in x 4½in rectangle to the top of this unit and press.

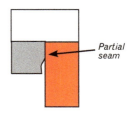

Partial seam

3 Sew a colour A 2½in x 4½in rectangle to the left side of this unit and press.

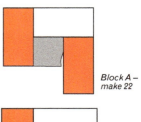

Block A – make 22

4 Sew a colour B 2½in x 4½in rectangle to the bottom and press. You can now complete the first partially sewn seam to complete the block. Press the seam. Repeat to make twenty-two of block A.

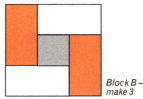

Block B – make 3

Making block B

5 Sew a 2½in x 6½in colour A rectangle to a 4½in x 6½in background rectangle. Repeat to make three of block B.

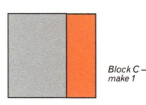

Block C – make 1

Making block C

6 Sew a 2½in x 6½in colour B rectangle to a 4½in x 6½in background rectangle to make of block C.

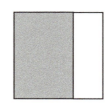

Making block D

7 Sew a 2½in x 4½in colour A rectangle to a 2½in x 4½in background rectangle and press. Sew a 2½in x 4½in colour B rectangle to the bottom of the unit and press.

8 Sew a 2½in x 6½in colour A rectangle on the right-hand side of the unit and press. Repeat to make six of block D.

Block D – make 6

Making block E

9 Sew a 2½in x 4½in colour B rectangle to a 2½in x 4½in background rectangle and press. Sew a 2½in x 4½in colour A rectangle to the bottom of the unit and press.

10 Sew a 2½in x 6½in colour B rectangle on the right-hand side of the unit to make one block E and press.

Block E – make 1

Making block F

11 Sew a 2½in x 4½in colour A rectangle to both sides of a 2½in x 4½in background rectangle and press. Sew a 2½in x 6½in colour B rectangle to the bottom to make one block F.

Making block G

12 Sew a 2½in x 4½in colour A rectangle to the bottom of a 4½in background square and then sew a 2½in x 6½in colour B rectangle on the right-hand side and press. Repeat to make five of block G.

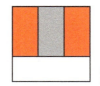

Block F – make 1

Block G – make 5

Making block H

13 Sew a 2½in x 4½in colour B rectangle to the bottom of a 4½in background square and then sew a 2½in x 6½in colour A rectangle to the right-hand side and press. Repeat to make five of block H.

Block H – make 5

Making block J

14 Draw a diagonal line from corner to corner on the wrong side of a Colour A 2½in square, or mark with a fold. With right sides together, lay the marked Colour A square on one corner of a 6½in background square, aligning the outer edges. Sew across the diagonal, using the marked diagonal line as the stitching line.

15 Open the square out and press towards the outside of the block. Trim the excess Colour A corner fabric. Do not trim the background square as although this creates a little more bulk, it does keep your work in shape. Repeat this on all four corners. Repeat to make ten of block J.

Block J – make 10

Making block K

16 Working with Colour B 2½in squares and using the same technique as in steps 14 and 15, make eight of block K.

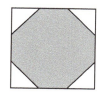

Block K – make 8

Making block L

17 Working with Colour A 2½in squares, and sewing only three corners, make six of block L.

Block L – make 6

Making block M

18 Working with Colour B 2½in squares, and sewing only three corners, make four of block M.

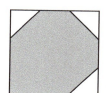

Block M – make 4

Making block N

19 Working with Colour A 2½in squares, and sewing only two corners, make two of block N.

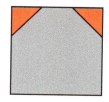

Block N – make 2

Making block O

20 Working with Colour B 2½in squares, and sewing only two corners, make six of block O.

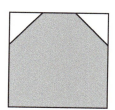

Block O – make 6

Making block P

21 Working with Colour A 2½in squares, and sewing only one corner, make two of block P.

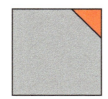

Block P –
make 2

Making block Q

22 Working with Colour B 2½in squares, and sewing only one corner, make eight of block Q.

Block Q –
make 8

When laying out all of the blocks, take your time to make sure all the blocks are in the correct positions before you begin sewing them together.

Assembling the quilt

23 Refer to the diagram and lay out the blocks into rows. When you are certain that you have everything in the correct place, sew the blocks into rows placing the 6½in background squares where shown on the diagram.

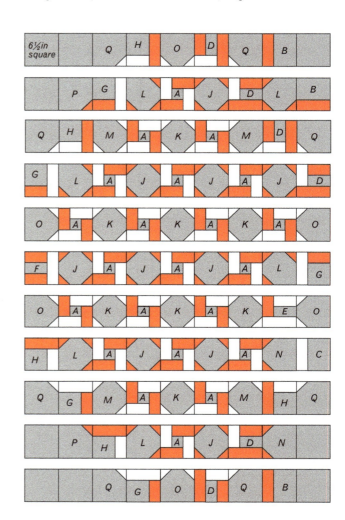

24 Sew the rows together, pinning at every seam intersection to ensure a perfect match. Your quilt top is now complete.

Quilting and finishing

25 You can now make a quilt sandwich as normal with your wadding (batting) and backing fabric, ready for quilting. Alternatively, you could piece the back of the quilt as we did by referring to the instructions that follow.

26 Sew the seven binding strips into a continuous length and bind the quilt to finish.

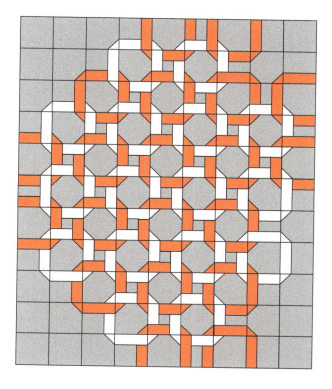

We chose a quilting design called Modern Beads and kept it dense at the start and end of the quilt and enlarged it towards the centre.

Making a Pieced Quilt Back

Cutting the backing fabric

1 Cut three 8½in strips across the width of the fabric and subcut two strips into four 8½in squares and cut the third strip into five 8½in squares. You need 42½in to do this so do not trim your selvedge too much. You need thirteen squares in total.

2 Cut two 11½in strips across the width of the fabric for the side borders. These need to be 42½in long.

3 Cut three 17½in strips across the width of the fabric for the top and bottom borders.

Assembling the backing

4 Using the twelve jelly roll strips, sew three strip units as shown and subcut each strip unit into sixteen 2½in segments to make a total of forty-eight segments.

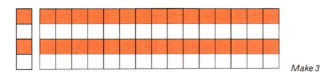

Make 3

5 Rotate half the segments 180 degrees and then sew the segments together to form twelve sixteen-patch blocks.

Make 12

6 Sew the sixteen-patch blocks together with the 8½in background squares to form rows. Sew the rows together, pinning at every seam intersection to ensure a perfect match.

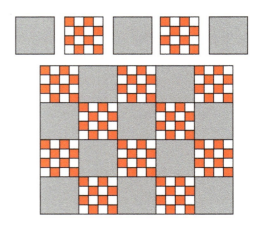

7 Sew on the 11½in wide side borders and press the seams outwards. Complete the quilt back by sewing the three 17½in strips into one continuous length. Trim to size and sew to the top and bottom of the quilt back.

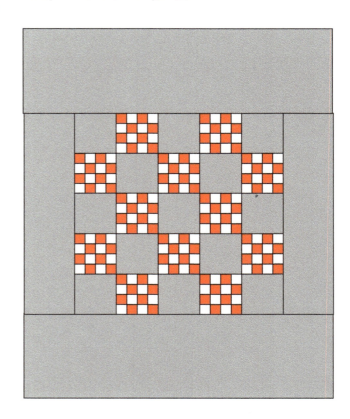

The reverse of this quilt uses a much more traditional design and here we have used our jelly roll strips to make some sixteen-patch blocks, setting them against a light grey print. Winter Wonderland from Moda is a very subtle Christmas range and if you look carefully you can see the occasional snowman. The quilt front and back were made by the authors and longarm quilted by The Quilt Room.

Log Cabin Sparkles

We used Heather Bailey's range Lottie Da for this quilt and our jelly roll contained two each of twenty of her gorgeous fabrics, which are the colours of exquisite Chinese porcelain. You do need your jelly roll strips to measure 42½in for this pattern so take care when trimming selvedges. Each jelly roll strip could be used to make one block but we preferred to make our quilt scrappy. We chose an aubergine colour for our accent fabric and used a selection of cream-on-cream fabrics for our background. As an alternative, a bright orange accent would look great, or a dark lime green.

We only had two jelly roll strips left over but this was just enough to make twelve Friendship Star blocks for the quilt back. We dotted these amongst a large floral fabric, which was also from the Lottie Da range.

Vital Statistics

Quilt size: 72in square

Block size: 12in square

Number of blocks: 36

Setting: 6 x 6 blocks

Requirements

For quilt top:

- One jelly roll **OR** forty assorted 2½in strips cut across the width of the fabric

- Background fabric 2¼yd (2.20m) **OR** for a scrappier effect an assortment of thirty-one 2½in strips cut across the width of the fabric

- Accent fabric 1¾yd (1.60m)

- Binding fabric ⅝yd (60cm)

- Creative Grids Multi-Size 45/90 ruler or other specialist ruler for making half-square triangles from strips

For pieced quilt back:

- Backing fabric 4½yd (4.25m)

- Two spare jelly roll strips

Log Cabin Sparkles Quilt

Preparation

Sorting the jelly roll strips:
- Choose thirty-six strips to make the dark 'logs' of the Log Cabin blocks.
- Choose two strips to make the half-square triangle units that form the off-centre square of each Log Cabin block.

Cutting the jelly roll strips:
You need your jelly roll strips to measure 42½in across the width of the fabric so do not be over enthusiastic in trimming the selvedges!
- Cut each of the thirty-six jelly roll strips allocated for the dark logs as follows.
  - One 2½in x 4½in rectangle.
  - One 2½in x 6½in rectangle.
  - One 2½in x 8½in rectangle.
  - One 2½in x 10½in rectangle.
  - One 2½in x 12½in rectangle.
- Leave the two strips allocated for the half-square triangles uncut for the moment.

Cutting the background fabric:
- Cut thirty-one 2½in strips across the width of the fabric and subcut as follows.
  - Take three and cut into thirty-six 2½in squares.
  - Take four and cut each into nine 2½in x 4½in rectangles to make a total of thirty-six.
  - Take six and cut each into six 2½in x 6½in rectangles to make a total of thirty-six.
  - Take nine and cut each into four 2½in x 8½in rectangles to make a total of thirty-six.
  - Take nine and cut each into four 2½in x 10½in rectangles to make a total of thirty-six.

Cutting the accent fabric:
- Cut twenty-three 2½in strips across the width of the fabric. Leave two uncut for making the half-square triangles.
- Take the other twenty-one strips and cut sixteen 2½in accent squares from each strip to make 336 in total.

Cutting the binding fabric:
- Cut eight 2½in strips across the width of the fabric.

Making the Quilt

Making the half-square triangle units

1 Take one of the jelly roll strips allocated for the half-square triangles and a 2½in accent strip and press right sides together, ensuring that they are exactly one on top of the other. The pressing will help hold the two strips together.

2 Lay them out on a cutting mat and position the Multi-Size 45/90 ruler as shown in the diagram, lining up the 2in mark at the bottom edge of the strips. Trim the selvedge and cut the first triangle. You will notice that the cut-out triangle has a flat top. This would just have been a dog ear you needed to cut off – so it's saving you time.

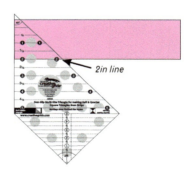

2in line

3 Rotate the ruler 180 degrees as shown and cut the next triangle. Continue along the strip to cut eighteen triangles.

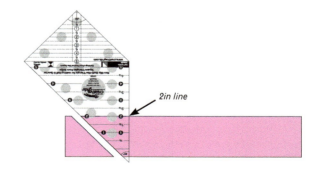

2in line

4 Sew along the diagonal of each pair of triangles. Trim the dog ears and press the seam towards the accent fabric to form eighteen half-square triangle units. Repeat with the other pair of strips allocated for the half-square triangles to make thirty-six in total.

 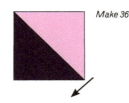

Make 36

Sewing the flip-over log corners

5 Draw a diagonal line from corner to corner on the wrong side of a 2½in accent square, or mark with a fold, and lay it on the corner of a 2½in x 4½in jelly roll log, aligning the outer edges as shown. Sew across the diagonal, using the marked diagonal line as the stitching line.

6 Open the square out and press towards the outside of the block. Trim the excess accent fabric. Do not trim the jelly roll log, as although this creates a little more bulk, it does keep your work in shape (see Tip). Repeat with all thirty-six 2½in x 4½in jelly roll logs.

*Make 36 –
2½in x 4½in*

Tip

If you prefer to reduce bulk and trim the jelly roll fabric as well, only do this after checking that your corner has been sewn on accurately.

7 Repeat steps 5 and 6 using the 2½in x 6½in jelly roll logs to make a total of thirty-six.

*Make 36 –
2½in x 6½in*

8 Repeat steps 5 and 6 using the 2½in x 8½in jelly roll logs, but this time sew a flip-over corner to the top and bottom of each log to make thirty-six in total.

*Make 36 –
2½in x 8½in*

9 Repeat steps 5 and 6 using the 2½in x 10½in jelly roll logs, but this time sew a flip-over corner to the top and bottom of each log to make thirty-six in total.

*Make 36 –
2½in x 10½in*

10 Repeat steps 5 and 6 using the 2½in x 12½in jelly roll logs, but this time sew a flip-over corner to the top and bottom of each log to make thirty-six in total.

*Make 36 –
2½in x 12½in*

11 Repeat steps 5 and 6 using a 2½in x 6½in background log, sewing the flip-over corner as shown to the bottom right corner. Repeat to make sixteen.

Make 16 –
2½in x 6½in

12 Repeat steps 5 and 6 using a 2½in x 8½in background log, sewing the flip-over corner to the bottom right corner. Repeat to make sixteen.

Make 16 –
2½in x 8½in

13 Repeat steps 5 and 6 using a 2½in x 10½in background log, sewing the flip-over corner to the bottom right corner. Repeat to make sixteen.

Make 16 –
2½in x 10½in

Assembling block A

14 Sew a 2½in background square to the bottom of a half-square triangle unit and press as shown.

15 Sew a 2½in x 4½in jelly roll log to the right-hand side and press as shown.

16 Sew a 2½in x 4½in background log to the bottom and press as shown.

17 Sew a 2½in x 6½in jelly roll log to the right-hand side and press as shown.

18 Using the 6½in, 8½ and 10½in background logs with the flip-over corners and the 8½in, 10½in and 12½in jelly roll logs with two flip-over corners, continue sewing the logs to the block. Refer to the diagram to make sure you are sewing the correct log in place.

19 Repeat this log cabin process to make a total of sixteen of Block A.

Block A – make 16

Assembling block B

20 Using the background logs without flip-over corners, and using the same log cabin process, make twenty of Block B.

Block B – make 20

We chose an intricate feather design that we quilted block by block, and then added a small apple core design in the solid aubergine squares.

Assembling the quilt

21 Lay out the blocks with the sixteen Block A in the centre of the quilt and the twenty Block B around the outside, making sure you position the blocks correctly. When you are happy everything is in the correct place, sew the blocks into rows. Sew the rows together, pinning at every seam intersection to ensure a perfect match. Your quilt top is now complete.

Quilting and finishing

22 You can now make a quilt sandwich as normal with your wadding (batting) and backing fabric, ready for quilting. Alternatively, you could piece the back of the quilt as we did by referring to the instructions that follow.

23 Sew the eight binding strips into a continuous length and bind the quilt to finish.

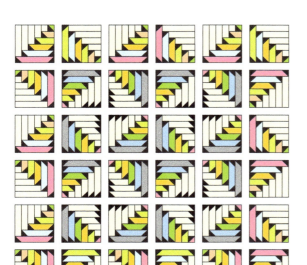

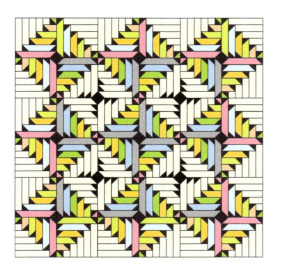

Making a Pieced Quilt Back

Cutting the backing fabric

1 Cut six 2½in strips, each cut across the full width of the backing fabric.
- Subcut four strips into sixty 2½in squares.
- Leave two strips uncut to make the half-square triangle units.

2 Cut four 6½in strips, each cut across the width of the backing fabric.
- Subcut two strips into twelve 6½in squares.
- Subcut two strips into four rectangles 6½in x 18½in.

3 Cut one length of 36½in and cut in half to create two rectangles 21in x 36½in.

4 Cut one length of 78½in and cut in half to create two rectangles 21in x 78½in.

Assembling the backing

5 Take the two jelly roll strips and two 2½in background strips and, using the Multi-Size 45/90 ruler, make forty-eight half-square triangle units.

Make 48

6 Sew these together with the 2½in background squares to make twelve Friendship Star blocks.

7 Sew three of the Friendship Star blocks together with three 6½in squares and one 6½in x 18½in rectangle as shown. Repeat to make four of these units.

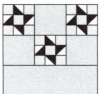

Make 4

8 Sew the four units together as shown and then add the border by sewing a 21in x 36½in rectangle to either side of the quilt and then the 21in x 78½in rectangles to the top and bottom to finish.

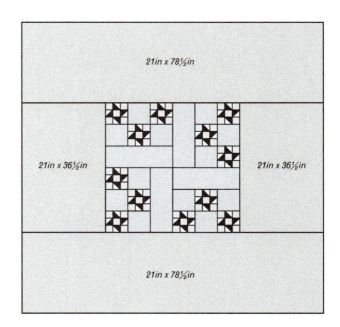

We only had two jelly roll strips left over for the reverse of this quilt so we made them into Friendship Star blocks and pieced them into a large floral fabric from the same range – Lottie Da by Heather Bailey. The quilt front and back were made by the authors and longarm quilted by The Quilt Room.

General Techniques

Tools

All the projects in this book require rotary cutting equipment. You will need a self-healing cutting mat at least 18in x 24in and a rotary cutter. We recommend the 45mm or the 60mm diameter rotary cutter. Any rotary cutting work requires rulers and most people have a make they prefer.

We like the Creative Grids rulers as their markings are clear, they do not slip on fabric and their Turn-a-Round facility is so useful when dealing with half-inch measurements. We recommend the 6½in x 24½in as a basic ruler plus a large square no less than 12½in, which is handy for squaring up and making sure you are always cutting at right angles.

In a number of the quilts in this book we have used a large 60-degree triangle that can measure up to 8in triangles and this is a great basic ruler to have in your collection. We used this ruler in the Diamond Drops, Ocean Deep, Hexagon Star and Firecracker quilts.

You need a speciality ruler for making half-square triangles from strips and the Multi-Size 45/90 or the Flying Geese 45/90 rulers can be used here. These rulers show the *finished* size measurements. This means that when you are cutting half-square triangles from 2½in strips you line up the 2in marking along the bottom of the strip to make 2in finished half-square triangles. If you are using a different ruler, please make sure you are lining up your work on the correct markings. The Flying Geese 45/90 ruler can also be used to make the Basket Weave quilt as a large 90-degree triangle is required for this.

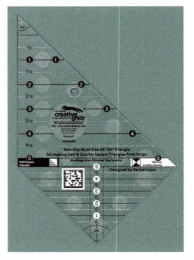

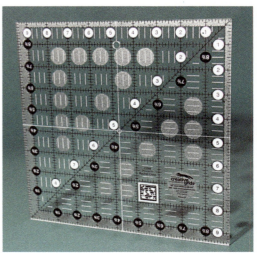

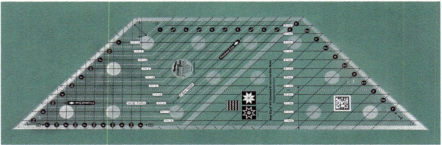

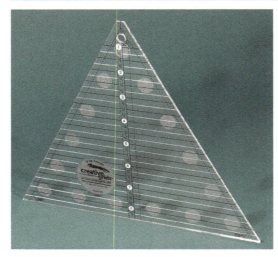

We quilters all have our favourite rulers. We like to use the Creative Grids rulers and squares, some of which are shown here, including the Multi-Size 45/90 and the 60-degree triangle.

Seams

We cannot stress enough the importance of maintaining an accurate ¼in seam allowance throughout. We prefer to say an accurate *scant* ¼in seam because there are two factors to take into account. Firstly, the thickness of thread and secondly, when the seam allowance is pressed to one side it takes up a tiny amount of fabric. These are both extremely small amounts but if they are ignored you will find your *exact* ¼in seam allowance is taking up more than ¼in. So, it is well worth testing your seam allowance before starting on a quilt and most sewing machines have various needle positions that can be used to make any adjustments.

Seam allowance test

Take a 2½in strip and cut off three segments each 1½in wide. Sew two segments together down the longer side and press the seam to one side. Sew the third segment across the top. It should fit exactly. If it doesn't, you need to make an adjustment to your seam allowance. If it is too long, your seam allowance is too wide and can be corrected by moving the needle on your sewing machine to the right. If it is too small, your seam allowance is too narrow and this can be corrected by moving the needle to the left.

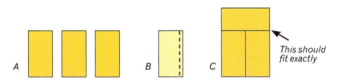

A   B   C

This should fit exactly

Pressing

In quilt making, pressing is of vital importance and if extra care is taken you will be well rewarded. This is especially true when dealing with strips. If your strips start bowing and stretching you will lose accuracy.

- Always set your seam after sewing by pressing the seam as sewn, without opening up your strips. This eases any tension and prevents the seam line from distorting. Move the iron with an up and down motion, zigzagging along the seam rather than ironing down the length of the seam, which could cause distortion.

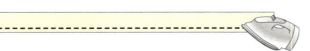

- Open up your strips and press on the *right* side of the fabric towards the darker fabric, if necessary guiding the seam underneath to make sure the seam is going in the right direction. Press with an up and down motion rather than along the length of the strip.

- Always take care if using steam and certainly don't use steam anywhere near a bias edge.

- When you are joining more than two strips together, press the seams after attaching each strip. This is because you are more likely to get bowing if you leave it until your strip unit is complete before pressing.

- Each seam must be pressed flat before another seam is sewn across it. Unless there is a special reason for not doing so, seams are pressed towards the darker fabric. The main criteria when joining seams, however, is to have the seam allowances going in the opposite direction to each other as they then nest together without bulk. Your patchwork will lie flat and your seam intersections will be accurate.

Pinning

Don't underestimate the benefits of pinning. When you have to align a seam it is important to insert pins to stop any movement when sewing. Long, fine pins with flat heads are recommended as they will go through the layers of fabric easily and allow you to sew up to and over them.

Seams should always be pressed in opposite directions so they will nest together nicely. Insert a pin either at right angles or diagonally through the seam intersection, ensuring that the seams are matching perfectly. When sewing, do not remove the pin too early as your fabric might shift and your seams will not be perfectly aligned.

Chain Piecing

Chain piecing is the technique of feeding a series of pieces through the sewing machine without lifting the presser foot and without cutting the thread between each piece. Always chain piece when you can – it saves time and thread. Once your chain is complete, snip the thread between the pieces.

When chain piecing shapes other than squares and rectangles it is sometimes preferable when finishing one shape, to lift the presser foot slightly and reposition on the next shape, still leaving the thread uncut.

Removing Dog Ears

A dog ear is the excess piece of fabric that overlaps past the seam allowance when sewing triangles to other shapes. Dog ears should always be cut off to reduce bulk. They can be trimmed using a rotary cutter, although snipping with small, sharp scissors is quicker. Make sure you are trimming the points parallel to the straight edge of the triangle.

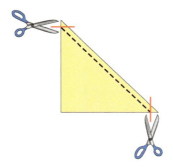

Joining Border and Binding Strips

If you need to join strips for your borders and binding, you may choose to join them with a diagonal seam to make them less noticeable. Press the seams open.

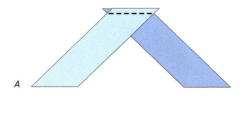

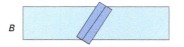

Adding Borders

The fabric requirements in this book all assume you are going to be sewing straight rather than mitred borders. If you intend to have mitred borders please add sufficient extra fabric for this.

Adding straight borders

1 Determine the vertical measurement from top to bottom through the centre of your quilt top. Cut two side border strips to this measurement. Mark the halves and quarters of one quilt side and one border with pins. Placing right sides together and matching the pins, stitch the quilt and border together, easing the quilt side to fit where necessary. Repeat on the opposite side. Press open.

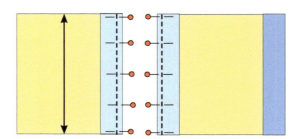

2 Determine the horizontal measurement from side to side across the centre of the quilt top. Cut two top and bottom border strips to this measurement and add to the quilt top in the same manner.

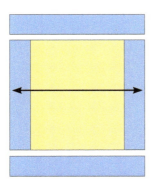

Adding mitred borders

If you wish to create mitred borders rather than straight borders follow these instructions.

1 Measure the length and width of the quilt and cut two border strips the length of the quilt *plus* twice the width of the border, and then cut two border strips the width of the quilt *plus* twice the width of the border.

2 Sew the border strips to the quilt beginning and ending ¼in away from the corners, backstitching to secure at either end. Begin your sewing right next to where you have finished sewing your previous border but ensure your stitching doesn't overlap. When you have sewn your four borders, press and lay the quilt out on a flat surface, the reverse side of the quilt up.

3 Fold the top border up and align it with the side border. Press the resulting 45-degree line that starts at the ¼in stop and runs to the outside edge of the border.

4 Now lift the side border above the top border and fold it to align with the top border. Press it to create a 45-degree line. Repeat with all four corners.

5 Align the horizontal and vertical borders in one corner by folding the quilt diagonally and stitching along the pressed 45-degree line to form the mitre, back stitching at either end. Trim the excess border fabric ¼in from your sewn line. Repeat with the other three corners.

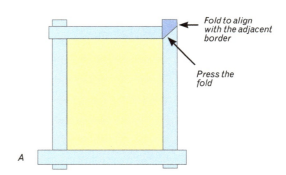

Fold to align with the adjacent border

Press the fold

A

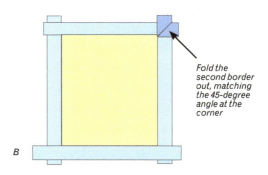

Fold the second border out, matching the 45-degree angle at the corner

B

Quilting

Quilting stitches hold the patchwork top, wadding (batting) and backing together and create texture over your finished patchwork. The choice is yours whether you hand quilt, machine quilt or send your quilt off to a longarm quilting service. There are many books dedicated to the techniques of hand and machine quilting but the basic procedure is as follows.

1 With the aid of templates or a ruler, mark out the quilting lines on the patchwork top.

2 Cut the backing fabric and wadding 4in larger all around than the patchwork top. Pin or tack (baste) the layers together to prepare them for quilting.

3 Quilt either by hand or by machine. Remove any quilting marks on completion of the quilting. Tie off and bury any thread ends in the wadding.

Binding a Quilt

The fabric requirements in this book are for a 2½in double-fold binding cut on the straight grain.

1 Trim the excess backing and wadding (batting) so that the edges are even with the top of the quilt.

2 Join your binding strips into a continuous length, making sure there is sufficient to go around the quilt plus 8in–10in for corners and overlapping ends. With wrong sides together, press the binding in half lengthways. Fold and press under ½in to neaten the edge at the end where you will start sewing.

3 On the right side of the quilt and starting about 12in away from a corner, align the edges of the double thickness binding with the edge of the quilt, so that the cut edges are towards the edges of the quilt, and pin to hold in place. Sew with a ¼in seam allowance, leaving the first inch open.

4 At the first corner, stop ¼in from the edge of the fabric and backstitch (see diagram A). Lift needle and presser foot. Fold the binding upwards and then downwards (B and C). Stitch from the edge to ¼in from the next corner and repeat the turn.

5 Continue all around the quilt working each corner in the same way. When you come to the starting point, cut the binding, fold under the cut edge and overlap at the starting point.

6 Fold the binding over to the back of the quilt and hand stitch in place, folding at each corner to form a neat mitre.

Making a Larger Quilt

If you want to make a larger version of any of the quilts in the book, refer to the Vital Statistics of the quilt, which shows the block size, the number of blocks, how the blocks are set plus the size of border used. You can then calculate your requirements for a larger quilt.

Calculating Backing Fabric

The majority of the quilt patterns in this book have pieced backings but if you want to have a plain backing as normal then the following information will be useful. Many people like to use extra-wide backing fabric so they do not need any seams.

Using 60in wide fabric

This is a simple calculation as to how much you need to buy. Example: your quilt is 54in x 72in. Your backing needs to be 3in larger all round so your backing measurement is 60in x 78in. If you have found 60in wide backing, then you would buy the length which is 78in. However, if you have 90in wide backing, you can turn it round and you would only have to buy the width of 60in.

Using 42in wide fabric

You will need to have a join or joins in order to get the required measurement unless the backing measurement for your quilt is 42in or less on one side. If your backing measurement is less than 42in then you need only buy one length.

Using the previous example, if your backing measurement is 60in x 78in, you will need one seam somewhere in your backing. If you join two lengths of 42in fabric together your new fabric measurement will be 84in (less a little for the seam). This would be enough for the length of the quilt, so you need to buy twice the width, i.e., 60in x 2 = 120in. Your seam will run horizontally.

If your quilt length is more than your new backing fabric measurement of 84in you will need to use the measurement of 84in for the width of your quilt and you will have to buy twice the length. Your seam will then run vertically.

Labelling Your Quilt

When you have finished your quilt it is important to label it, even if the information you put on the label is just your name and the date. When looking at antique quilts it is always interesting to piece together information about the quilt, so you can be sure that any extra information you put on the label will be of immense interest to quilters of the future. You could say why you made the quilt and who it was for, or for what special occasion. Labels can be as ornate as you like, but a very simple and quick method is to write on a piece of calico with a permanent marker pen and then appliqué this to the back of your quilt.

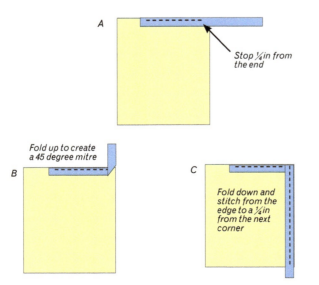

A

Stop ¼in from the end

Fold up to create a 45 degree mitre

B

C

Fold down and stitch from the edge to a ¼in from the next corner

Useful Contacts

The Quilt Room
(Shop, Mail Order and Gammill UK Dealers)
37–39 High Street, Dorking, Surrey RH4 1AR, UK
Tel: 01306 877307
www.quiltroom.co.uk

Creative Grids (UK) Ltd
23A Pate Road, Melton Mowbray,
Leicestershire LE13 0RG, UK
Tel: 01455 828667
www.creativegrids.com

Gammill Inc
1452 W. Gibson, West Plains, MO. 65775, USA
www.gammill.net

Janome UK Ltd
Janome Centre, Southside, Stockport, Cheshire SK6 2SP, UK
Tel: 0161 666 6011
www.janome.com

Moda Fabrics/United Notions
13800 Hutton Drive, Dallas, Texas 75234, USA
Tel. 800-527-9447
www.modafabrics.com

About the Authors

Pam Lintott opened her quilt shop, The Quilt Room, in 1981, which she still runs today, along with her daughter Nicky. Pam is the author of *The Quilt Room Patchwork & Quilting Workshops,* as well as *The Quilter's Workbook.* The shop together with the mail order department and longarm quilting department are housed in a 15th century inn located in the historic market town of Dorking, Surrey just south of London, UK.

New Ways with Jelly Rolls is Pam and Nicky's eleventh book for David & Charles following on from *Dessert Roll Quilts* and *Quick Quilts with Rulers* and their eight extremely successful Jelly Roll Quilt books including the phenomenally successful *Jelly Roll Quilts.*

Acknowledgments

Pam and Nicky would firstly like to thank Mark Dunn and the whole team at Moda Fabrics for their continued support and for allowing them to use the name Jelly Roll in the title and throughout the book. Thanks to Janome Sewing Machines for allowing Pam and Nicky the use of their reliable sewing machines when making up the quilts for this book. Thanks to the girls at The Quilt Room – shop, mail order and the longarm department – who keep The Quilt Room running smoothly when Pam and Nicky are rushing to meet tight deadlines.

Extra special thanks to Pam's husband Nick and to Nicky's husband Rob for looking after everything that needs to be done when deadlines are being met and computers and sewing machines are working overtime! Last, but not least, a special thank you to Freddie (now four) who has grown up thinking that everyone is surrounded by piles of quilts and, like his mother and nanna, it is quite usual for people to be always covered in threads!

Index

A DAVID & CHARLES BOOK
© F&W Media International, Ltd 2014

David & Charles is an imprint of F&W Media International, Ltd
Pynes Hill Court, Pynes Hill, Exeter, EX2 5AZ, UK

F&W Media International, Ltd is a subsidiary of F+W Media, Inc
10151 Carver Road, Suite #200, Blue Ash, OH 45242, USA

Text and Designs © Pam and Nicky Lintott 2014
Layout and Photography © F&W Media International, Ltd 2014

First published in the UK and USA in 2014

Pam and Nicky Lintott have asserted their right to be identied as authors of this work
in accordance with the Copyright, Designs and Patents Act, 1988.

A catalogue record for this book is available from the British Library.

ISBN-13: 978-1-4463-0476-1 paperback
ISBN-10: 1-4463-0476-0 paperback

ISBN-13: 978-1-4463-1153-0 hardcover
ISBN-10: 1-4463-1153-8 hardcover

F&W Media International, Ltd
Pynes Hill Court, Pynes Hill, Exeter, EX2 5AZ, UK

10 9 8 7 6 5 4

Acquisitions Editor: Sarah Callard
Editor: Matthew Hutchings
Project Editor: Lin Clements
Art Editor: Jodie Lystor
Photographers: Jack Kirby and Jack Gorman
Senior Production Controller: Kelly Smith

F+W Media publishes high quality books on a wide range of subjects.
For more great book ideas visit: www.sewandso.co.uk

www.ingramcontent.com/pod-product-compliance
Ingram Content Group UK Ltd.
Pitfield, Milton Keynes, MK11 3LW, UK
UKHW050509120625
459556UK00002B/3